Flickering

Flickering

GERRY HUERTH

LitPrime Solutions
21250 Hawthorne Blvd
Suite 500, Torrance, CA 90503
www.litprime.com
Phone: 1-800-981-9893

Published by LitPrime Solutions: 09/01/2023

ISBN: 979-8-88703-293-1(sc)
ISBN: 979-8-88703-294-8(e)

Library of Congress Control Number: 2023916767

Contents

Chapter 1

That night, four months after Gizmo the dog died, he sat, his face a cool moon reflecting the light from the solitary lamp, a light so meager that it left the darkness of the room intact and deep. His eyes frozen in stillness stared at the green and blue hummingbirds delicately painted on the white ceramic lamp. Ever so subtly his nostrils and the very tip of his nose twitched. His eyes, resisting the agitation, fixed more intensely on those fragile hummingbirds frozen in time. The creases around his eyes deepened with strain. Then, powered by some unexpected surge of electricity, his right hand hitherto lying on his lap, clenched and motionless like a clod, suddenly jabbed upward, fingers unfolding, jittery as spider legs; and reached towards his face.

As those spider legs continued scrambling over his nose, the contortions of his face diminished to stillness. The hand, his hand, as suddenly as it arrived on his face, now returned to its place on his lap. Once again his face frozen in a timeless stare, fixed again on those hummingbirds painted on the lamp that Sheila, who now calls herself Presence, gave him when she somehow knew it was time to sell all her possessions to go on the road.

How do things actually happen in time? No one ever really ponders time, contenting themselves with a blur of clichés. The intense focus of his face began drooping in complaint. People were sure after all, and for the longest time, that the earth beneath their feet flattened into a plain with edges, edges. A smile flickered on his face. It wasn't stupidity really; the explanations, reasons, rules, and predictions that sustained this tableau were elaborate and clever; perhaps it was just a lack of imagination. He nodded tolerantly. People are so oblivious to mystery, waking up in the morning, clothing themselves in their strategies to fend off chaos, drinking their first cups of coffee to impel them through the day; without ever considering if that Time Clock that propelled them into action might be less substantial than the steam rising from those same coffee cups. He once again fixed his eyes so fiercely on that lamp that those birds almost seemed to quiver. Perhaps that old Greek Zeno had it right; motion through time is a figment of our imagination, an absurd but strangely useful convention

He stared motionless, a bird watcher, caught in the suspense of waiting, yearning, despite the absurdity; for the scene to come to life and move with the magic of living creatures breathing and perhaps even looking back. After all, without motion and time, he was frozen, alone, like a figure in a Greek Icon, staring out from mystery.

Despite his quandary, his breaths picked up momentum, chest rising and falling in imagined but preposterous hope of communicating with other beings, even if feathered and painted on porcelain. He half closed his eyes yearning for some new paradigm that would allow those birds to take flight; a little twitch would do: a paradigm that would allow for some kind of response from the outside but would still guarantee his safety. Silent night, holy night and all that lullaby of yearning.

Stories he had aplenty, those images flickering on the insides of his eyeballs, still pictures flying by so quickly that they gave the illusion of life and breath. No one really believes that stuff, just stories for children who don't want to feel alone, who want to believe in reward and punishment; stories like little universes of time all neatly strung out into a semblance of beginning, middle, and end: strung like beads. That's too decoratively benign a notion: a conveyor belt...that's better...grinding away and pulling us through all our wishes and terrors. He glanced away from the lamp into a dark corner of the living room. His left heel throbbed; the chiropractor said that with age and wear and tear the bones of his feet were shifting--how's that for a story? He stretched his leg out rotating his ankle in a circle. Such foolishness! He jabbed the lamp with a scolding glance.

He stood up, his drooping form escaping the halo of the lamp. With the solemn look of a Christian virgin, stepping into a lion infested Roman coliseum; he faced the dark conveyor belt of a winter night in Minnesota and took a step. He could almost see tomorrow.

Walking toward the dark kitchen his steps slowed with the ambivalence of people traveling those moving walkways at airports...should they step toward their destination or simply let the belt move them? He surprised himself when his hand flicked on the light switch in the kitchen and brightness exploded in his face. He stood motionless taking in the illumination... like Paul on the road to Damascus.

Opening a cupboard he grabbed a couple of cans and a cellophane bag of dried egg noodles. He pulled a clanging pan from beneath the sink, filled it with the waterfall from the faucet and placed it on the stove. Turning a little knob to the left, flames flashed on under the pot. He paused as if he had just slipped off the belt... bewildered by the mystery of fire. His body quivered slightly resisting the sense of wonder...those little blue flames dancing around the metal circle: fire, motion, time; he pondered. Then grimacing with determination he walked to the counter, sliding open a drawer and pulled out a can opener. During some yesterday of his imagination, he had presumably placed it there. What is even more amazing, he remembered that location from a past that is only imagined.

The conveyor belt must have moved on; in one hand he found himself carrying a ceramic casserole filled with slithery noodles and white glop, and with the other hand he opened the complaining oven door. His body arched downward in a genuflection and pushed the casserole across the wire grate and into the inferno... yes, even hell provides coordinates to confusion. Eyes once again focused on cosmic questions, his body moved toward the sink. A small mound of suds stubbornly floated there, persisting, even though the water had been drawn in some earlier reincarnation of the past. The cold dark winter seeped through the walls of the old house; his hands sought refuge in the warm sudsy bath. As they slowly swished through the silky comfort, his face relaxed as he slipped into memories and other fancies. Not a bad day...other than accidentally wearing two different shoes to college. His students seemed strangely understanding, hardly glancing at each. Perhaps being more bereft of coordinates than he, they drew some comfort from his confusion. College is so full of people not knowing how to get to a place that they haven't dared imagine. His hands moved through the water caressing the dishes in luxurious relief.

And then, another universe: he stood, hand in the still warm water, the dirty dishes that had been immersed in the sudsy sink had deposited themselves on the wire dish rack which rested serenely on the counter. A task completed; he pondered the mystery of it all as the furnace huffed on anxiously. With some embarrassment he jerked his hands out of the water, drying them on his pant pockets. He turned and stared out the black frosted window of the future.

Something exploded in his ears, a Big Bang blossoming in his reverie: the phone ringing rippling out into the confines of the house...something unexpected. His eyes expanded in shock, his chest pumping. His hands grasped the edge of the sink for reassurance, steadying himself.

He took a deep desperate gulp of air and walked toward that exploding sound, the Big Bang. He pondered that if there was no space and time prior to that explosive moment, there was no where or when for it to occur.

He picked up the receiver, "Hello..."

"It's Presence." Her voice punched out the syllables and stopped abruptly at the drop off, waiting for someone below to catch her.

His voice paused a little too long; timing is everything. "Shei...Presence, how are you doing...nice to hear from you."

She sounded disappointed for an instant and then her voice picked up its more rapid fire pace, "I'm in northern California. I parked my van at a commune that I heard about. You wouldn't believe what I'm doing.

Hesitantly, "I wouldn't?"

"I'm drinking a beer and listening to the sound of rain hitting the roof of the van."

"You are? That sounds fun." Thomas's eye stared out into an imagined distance. His shoulders jerked as he roused himself, mustering more enthusiasm. "Yes." He said more emphatically.

The enthusiasm was adequate. "I met a man."

"A man?"

"He's a plumber. He hasn't had sex for years. He likes me."

"Do you like him, The Plumber?"

Through the receiver Thomas heard distant car wheels rolling over gravel.

"But it's not going to stop my trip." Her voiced punched out the words defiantly.

Thomas heard the sound of car tires on gravel suddenly stop.

Her voice picked up urgent momentum. "That's him pulling up."

"That sounds exciting." He knew he sounded too bland.

"When are you going to visit me?"

For an instant Thomas looked around the room like a cornered rat; he hated being put on the spot. Through the receiver Thomas heard the sound of a door being knocked on insistently.

Presence's voice sounded frantic as if she were sending some last message before her impending death. "I'm going to be in Tucson the last two weeks of December."

In the face of such dire need Thomas mustered an answer, "I'll see; I have a friend, Joe, Joe...the guy I lived with in New York. I might...maybe I could stay there. And Danny could find a cheap flight for me."

"Gotta run, see ya in Tucson...call me to let me know for sure."

"I have some time off." He heard the phone disconnect abruptly.

Thomas sat holding the phone as it hummed. He looked up, frowned a little and gently set the phone down on the receiver. His face smoothed out in a mask of calmness; the mask allowed him the stolen luxury of being submerged in a shallow rippling pool of safety, even if it was self-imposed and fragile: a car whirring by on the street, the hum of the furnace, a plane in the distance: the pulsing sound of night. His face scrunched into a tight frown. The shallow pool evaporated--he promised Presence he would come to Arizona. He pondered: time doesn't run smoothly, the moments explode, where and when continues to be a mystery.

The sound of the porch door opening jerked him back onto the conveyor belt of a cold winter night: footsteps across the porch, the storm door opening, the sound of keys jingling in the lock of the front door, the door pushed open, a head sticking in, "Hi honey, I'm home."

Thomas, bewildered, looked toward the intruding sound, establishing quadrants in nowhere.

Danny closed the door behind him peering expectantly into the room: watery blue eyes searching for something. His eyes found Thomas. Danny flashed a smile at his audience of one. "I talked with Bud...he said he found a place for the winter...at a farm up near Rogers...the owner trains horses."

Thomas swallowed, his face flattening in an approximation of composure, his eyes focusing on Danny, not Danny's face exactly, but slightly over his shoulder. "Hi honey. Bud?"

"BUD," Danny repeated emphatically, an edge of irritation in his voice.

"Bud, Bud, oh ya, that Bud."

"A sweet deal! There's a small apartment in the house that's not being used. Bud will be in heaven…heat and warm water…no more shitting into newspapers…a toilet."

"Heaven." Thomas was getting into the swing of the conversation.

Danny placed a pile of mail on the dining room table, leaving his hands free to direct the scene. "Shitting in newspapers! He's coming over after church on Sunday."

"Guess he won't need to shower here anymore, of course unless he needs to."

"Heaven with all the trimmings."

The two made eye contact in a flickering moment of connection.

Danny's faced relaxed, his eyes especially. "I talked with Joan. Genevieve decided she doesn't want to be tube fed anymore."

Thomas looked bewildered: Genevieve…Genevieve… no illumination.

Danny's voice tightened. "You know, my Aunt Genevieve."

Thomas saw the light. "Oh ya."

Danny frowned.

Thomas prodded his relief into a look of concern. "Will the family let her do it?"

You know how Genevieve is. She hasn't been able

to swallow anything for weeks. Joan does the tube-feedings. Jim…you met Jim last summer…came over."

Thomas looked bewildered again.

"The son from Maplewood."

Thomas nodded reassuringly.

The momentum of Danny's story could build now. "Genevieve looked at Joan and Jim and said she wanted to stop the tube feedings. They asked her if that's what she really wanted. She said 'yes'."

Thomas's eyes blinked behind his glasses. He focused in on Danny's face with…flickering.

Danny's story moved on. "She could have stayed away from our wedding. Being ninety was a good enough excuse."

"Being ninety…" Thomas' voice trailed off. Once against he was far away in the contemplation of time.

"That's Genevieve." Danny's eyes searched Thomas' face. "It won't be long now."

Thomas came back from the distance; he wanted to supply some kind of coordinates for Danny's sadness. "You know with some people, it seems they chase around like they're afraid of running out of time or something. Genevieve…something about Genevieve…like she was really there, listening." He looked away.

The moment of connection between the two evaporated.

Danny loosened his tie impatiently. His face drooped in fatigue and vague complaint, sixty five years of pleasing wealthy donors was weighing him down. He headed towards the bedroom, his voice trailing behind him. "Rotary was boring. I don't know why speakers can't look up at their audiences. I sat next to Elizabeth. When is she going to get a clue? She was managing a fund raising event and even an idiot knows…"

His voice faded submerged in the sound of coat hangers chiming in the bedroom closet.

Thomas stared in the general direction of the racket. "Sheila…I mean Presence just called."

The racket in the closet stopped. "What?"

Thomas stood up and focused his attention. "Presence just called."

Danny stuck his head into the hallway of the dining room. "What does she want? Life on the road too much for her?"

Thomas's face tightened defensively. "She's doing fine."

"You'd think she never left the way she calls."

"She's in California, and it's raining."

Danny loved stories. "So what's new with her?"

"Oh I don't know…she seems all right. She met this guy."

"That'll be the end of her trip. Is she sleeping with him?"

"It won't." Thomas's face looked determined.

Danny turned back toward the bedroom.

Thomas focused on the back of Danny's neck. "Maybe, could you help me with something?"

Danny turned back to Thomas; the possibility of being a knight in shining armor dawned. His face shimmered with boyish eagerness. "What can I do for you?"

Thomas frowned, a struggle taking place in his imagination. He worked the frown into a smile. "You see Presence is going to be in Tucson the end of December and I was thinking of meeting her there. I have some time off and…"

Danny, clad only in underwear, spoke with the professional enthusiasm of a born promoter. "Sure, I'll get on the net and see about cheap flights."

Like an afterthought Thomas glanced at Danny, "Do you want to come?"

Danny's enthusiasm suddenly deflated. "You know I can't go. I just started working; I don't have vacation until March."

Thomas forced a smile of sympathy.

"Where would you stay out there?"

"I was thinking that maybe Joe might let me stay with him."

The story wasn't turning out the way Danny had anticipated. "Why don't you go on a vacation for once and not stay with someone?"

Thomas' body froze in stubborn resistance, but his voice still maintained his tone of supplication. "I don't have much money…it'll be okay with Joe…I think." Thomas pleaded his case. For an instant he wondered at the source of his determination.

Danny walked back into the bedroom. "It's not everybody who would find a ticket for his partner to go visit an old lover."

"It's not like that. We split up 25 years ago…my choice, sort of."

"Ya?" Danny's voice sounded skeptical.

Thomas's front teeth pressed against his lower lip…Presence, Joe, Danny…the stories and possibilities flashed on the inside of his eyeballs…a stream of still lives stretched out in front of him…The Big Bang…a new universes, boing born creating time and space. Eyes wide open, he took a deep breath. "I want to see Presence."

There was a moment of silence.

"Okay, okay" echoed from the bedroom.

Chapter 2

T homas sat at the dining room table, the cold seeping up from the dark basement through the old wooden floor and finally penetrating the soles of his shoes. His heels softly but persistently knocked together as if, like Dorothy of Oz, that repeated motion could transport him, if not to Kansas, at least via the magic of the telephone, to Tucson. He took a deep determined breath. His left hand slowly reached for the receiver while the right hand positioned itself over the keyboard of the old phone. The nervous fingers of his right hand hovered like a flock of little birds over the dialing pad. The birds began landing on those numbered and lettered buttons. In a remarkable feat of physical coordination his left hand delicately pressed the receiver against his ear.

The sound of ringing…one…two…three…Thomas's face was beginning to relax in disappointed relief. The fourth ring was abruptly interrupted by an irritated sounding voice, "Hello."

Thomas looked lost for an instant; finally against his better judgment he jumped in. "Hi Joe?" He smiled like an idiot.

"Look who's calling."

There was a pause as Thomas was trying to understand how he got into this situation. The wildness in his eyes diminished. "How are you?" The ball was in Joe's court now.

Silence on other end of the line; Joe never did like to talk on the phone especially about himself. "I'm drunk and broke."

"Oh." Thomas pondered that; Joe, always fearful of the envy of the gods, gave as little information about himself as possible. Thomas frowned; it was such a fine balance with Joe. He didn't want sympathy, praise, and definitely not affection, but he did want something though that never quite came to the surface.

"I'm a mess." Joe reiterated.

Against his better judgment Thomas tried sympathy. "That's too bad; are you all right?"

Silence on the other end of the line.

Joe made the faintest of noises, a kind of high-pitched humming sound.

That funny little note crossed thousands of miles and penetrated Thomas' ear, and before he knew it, relief, almost happiness warmed his cold toes. "Joe."

Joe's voice cooed back, "Pigface."

The miracle of the telephone crossed space and time.

Thomas spoke without thinking. " I'm your friend, always."

"I don't deserve you."

There was a long pause; Thomas wondered about memories; maybe they didn't have so much to do with time…maybe they hover around like dreamy angels, or maybe like the invisible flicker of hummingbird wings… we can't see them but we know they're there. His face had a faraway look.

Joe's voice broke the silence. "How are you Fuckface?"

Thomas felt the air stirred by wings. "So you're doing pretty well."

"I finally have a gallery for my work." Joe's voice relaxed, a message conveyed and received.

"Aw, that's great!" Thomas meant it. "Are you happy about it?"

"Me, happy?"

They both laughed.

Thomas's face tensed. "I want to ask you something."

"Fire away."

Thomas looked relieved. "I'd, I'd like to ask a favor. You can say no, and really, really, it'll be okay." His voice trailed off into helplessness.

Joe always felt safer when Thomas seemed helpless, "Sure."

"Well, I have some time toward the end of December off, and Danny can't come because of his job, and my friend Presence is riding around the West Coast, and I wondered if I could visit you and maybe meet up with her in Tucson.

No pause. "Sure come on down. I even have a spare bedroom."

Thomas looked like a child on Christmas morning. "She has some sort of live in van. I mean you don't have to..."

"Sure come on. She can park in the driveway and use my shower. I'll show you the gallery."

"You would?" Thomas stopped hitting his heels together.

"Stupid paintings...what day will you becoming?"

"December 28th."

Now there was a pause, static in the world of angels.

"If that's a problem, I don't have to come."

"I want you to come."

All clear.

Joe's voice sounded reassuring. "I'll just be getting back from Tacoma. I'll give you Richard's number to call, in case I'm not here yet."

"Richard?" Thomas looked worried.

"Richard, he's part of that couple I told you about."

Long pause...Thomas stared into his fluttering memory trying to place the name. Wings started appearing. He smiled, relishing his accomplishment. "The two guys you've been seeing...that Richard."

"I'm a whore."

Thomas basking in the accomplishment of his memory was too pleased to see anybody, especially Joe being punished. "You don't have to do that...as long as you're happy."

"Who said I was happy?"

"Oh, you know what I mean…if you're having good sex. It's what you always wanted. Are you sure he won't mind?"

"He'd like to."

"But what if…"

"You don't have to do that; come on down."

Thomas cradled the phone after the connection broke…he couple, yes, the couple…those two guys Joe was seeing…the couple…they found orifices Joe said he didn't even know he had.

Chapter 3

Thomas woke up several times that very same night, each time with a dream that he couldn't quite remember and each time he would fall asleep again. As an ashy winter dawn began creating shadowy dimension in the room, he turned onto his back, falling asleep, staring up at the ceiling, a murky movie screen for dreams. His closed eyes staring into the gray, unconsciousness hanging above his face. Starting in his stomach, waves of grief and guilt, especially guilt, begin rolling through his awareness.

In the distance he sees two pale people sitting on the seats of a movie theater; he knows that they are grieving parents and that somehow he is responsible for their grief. He can't look away; there is a tide, irresistibly pulling him toward the inconsolable couple. Now their faces like huge pale moons on the horizon of night, stare at him with frozen grief. Tears begin flowing from the craters of their eyes. The shadowy curtains of the movie theater begin to slowly part. A small glowing shape steps through the opening of the curtains and onto the stage and into Thomas' reluctant view...it is the girl...The Girl. In some terrible Annunciation, a fluttering dream angel proclaims that this is The Girl he, Thomas, has killed.

The shock woke him. His necked ached slightly as he blinked his eyes awake; the warm bed, the dark shape of the bureau with its pile of shadowy clothes on top: .a dream, only a dream. He tried to smile--a dream is nothing after all--he felt a drop of wetness on his cheek slowing flow down to be absorbed by the pillow beneath his head.

His body relaxed as gravity pushed him back into the shadowy mattress and sleep back into the mystery of dreamland. He hears the footsteps, soft, pattering little footsteps, starting faintly at first from out in the hallway, insistent as the sound of rain. The Dream Angel whispers that The Girl is approaches. Awareness...he can't close his eyes as he stares upward like a sacrificial victim. The steps came closer, almost to the edge of the bed now. Terrible retribution approaches. The gravity forces his eyelids further and further apart into a wild stare. His mouth opens into a great "O" of a silent scream, all frozen except for the throbbing pounding of his sacrificial blood.

The Girl hums a deep melody that seeps into his imagination, softening the nightmare. Like a spring shower, that penetrating warm rain of melody begins releasing his fears; his body begins letting go. The little footsteps approach: The Girl draws near for some reason: what does she want? A message, an order, some imagined possibility? In a dream transfiguration he is now a butterfly; his arms become wings, not wings for flight or escape, wings for ecstasy. She is at the edge of the bed now; the child not of doom but promise: The Girl.

Awakened, he felt the slightest swirl of air across his face. He found himself in this room with morning dawning in the window; the gentle message of The Girl's message fading into some inner knowing. What is it that he knows now? He lay awake wondering.

Danny's voice sleepily called out. "Are you all right?"

All right; the shapes in the room are objects again, part of a more familiar universe of space and time, but that knowing...he is knowing something...not a thing...a presence. He glanced over at Danny.

Danny raising his pale moon of a face, looked over at Thomas with concern.

Thomas still staring at the ceiling whispers, "I'm all right...a dream.." Thomas smiled, just enough to give reassurance, and then turned on his side toward Danny. "Where do dreams come from?"

Concern flashed then faded across Danny's face. "Tom, are you all right?' Danny's voice pleaded softly for the status quo of another morning.

Thomas turned, pressing his forehead against Danny's shoulder. "I'm alright. I just had this strange dream about a girl that died and then seemed to rise again."

Danny's hand rubbed Thomas' shoulder trying to erase the trouble. "It was only a dream."

"That's what they all say."

Chapter 4

Once again Thomas stood over a sink filled with dirty dishes. With both hands he picked up the plastic squeeze bottle of dish detergent, not that sex had ever been very satisfying for him. Sure there were those moments, when he was three and he saw his first Tarzan movie, that innocent face and torso glistening in the tropical sun of that black and white movie: an apparition. And of course with the men he had known since then, flesh and blood, they were as fleeting as the flickering television images, apparitions too. It wasn't that the actual men disappeared, but the feeling, the wonder, the splendor flickered then disappeared unsubstantial as a dream…something was missing.

His fingers softly squeezed the plastic container; only air came out. Maybe he was the apparition, and those unsubstantial dreams were all alive and breathing.

He shook his head slightly, maybe not Tarzan. He roused himself and with renewed determination and agin squeezed the detergent bottle. A few drops of viscous liquid spurted out and onto the side of the sink, midway down. A sour lemony smell penetrated his nose. The liquid slithered down the side of the sink slowly as a slug; he frowned. He had lived so much of his life trying to experience the world but always he was only left with longing. Maybe Time is the measure of longing; that's why it is so insistent. Immortal Tarzan or fickle flesh; time or presence, which comes first, which is more primary? Did god create man, or man create god, there's probably only room for one of the alternatives. Or maybe the real issue is the word "create," as if it's a being, a presence, like the strange melody, yes, The Girl. Maybe geography is misleading. A litany of men's names flashed across his mind, a sequence marking the passing of his life; with each name, hope had dawned briefly, fitfully; and then lost substance. He frowned. What is he missing? Or even more important: what's present. What's with the fractal pattern of longing?

Thomas took a deep breath and turned on the faucet over the sink. The faucet coughed and then a sputtering stream of water ran into the sink. When he first met Joe, Thomas had prayed, bargaining that he would give up everything if Joe would love him, and Joe did… sort of. For a few weeks there was an uneasy peace in the universe. Thomas felt alive, breathing, sometimes even laughing; and Joe was there. Thomas could feel the warmth of Joe's body and could smell the spicy deodorant mixed with earthy, sweat, not sour really.

The water, now steaming, was reaching the glob of dish detergent. Then Tarzan and the world of the flesh began separating as mutually exclusive things do.

Somewhere around the ending of the first month that he and Joe were together, a rift in the universe started opening. Thomas was trying to be the apparition of what Joe wanted: anything to stay with him. After all Joe was the apparition of Thomas' hopes. But peeking through the rift Thomas began to see that try as Joe might, he couldn't make Thomas the apparition of his hopes. Joe began having affairs. On the brink of chaos, Thomas kept wondering why he couldn't be what Joe wanted? What was wrong with him? For the next ten years both of them kept trying and missing, developing a strange forlorn understanding of each other. By the time Thomas ended the standoff...he turned off the water faucet.

He watched the white mounding bubbles float in the sink and shook his head, but Joe was aging too now. The last time Thomas saw Joe, his hair was graying and he had crinkling lines around his eyes. Thomas nodding reassuringly at the suds; the relationship was so much simpler now, two people, no apparitions, what a strange proposition! No disappointments and no punishments.

He piled dishes into the sink. Then there was Danny; at first Thomas felt a glimmer of longing with Danny. He seemed charming, outgoing, a faded leader of the pack, but Danny had an undertone of complaint in his voice. Danny was Danny with all his disappointments. What happened to Tarzan? Where do bubbles go when the soapy membrane bursts?

Thomas stared into the sparkling mound of bursting bubbles; John, what about John the Camper? Slowly with his left hand Thomas reached toward a sponge sitting on the counter. His hand dipped it into the sudsy water. His right hand fished a purple glass out of the suds; hands, sponge and glass swirled above the sink, water and suds dripping down, softly splashing...John... the conference in San Francisco, Thomas stumbled into that too, an education conference that his dean at college suggested he attend. Thomas knew he should attend, really.

Two weeks after that suggestion he found himself at a reception in a fancy hotel two thousand miles from home in San Francisco, surrounded by benign looking people who all seemed to be talking about teaching. The conference was on something called "Active Learning." He joined that eager pack. He smiled and took notes and tried to nod at the appropriate times. When anyone asked him a question, he tried to look as thoughtful as he could. He didn't even really understand the language; the attendees seemed to speak some language related to English, but somehow different, as if they all had come from some remote valley in Appalachia and had developed their own version of English. It occurred to Thomas with some embarrassment that maybe he was the one speaking the exotic dialect. Thomas was gradually becoming aware of a funny feeling in his stomach. A question surfaced; how come people are talking about active learning which engages students actively exploring, when most of the meetings were presented in Power Points, with the audience passively watching. What was the real message? Thomas, who was so used to absurdities watched his questions hover around him like hummingbirds or angels.

People seemed so pleased with themselves; he took it for granted that they understood each other. There seemed to be key words and phrases that people would mutter. Those key words would be displayed via Power Point screens during the workshops.

Nodding in sync with the other attendees, he saw a strange looking young man picking his way through the audience, a knapsack on his back. The young man wasn't nodding. Thomas studied The Camper. For a male his hips were a little broad and the hand with which he adjusted the knapsack seemed small. Something about his face: a pleasant face, a little incongruously boyish. Something about The Camper Thomas liked.

Thomas now glanced at the clean, wet dishes neatly arranged on the dish rack by the sink. His hands, governed by some independent force, once again entered the sudsy water searching for the last of the silverware.

The afternoon of the first day of the conference Thomas wandered into a small workshop session and sat down, a couple of seats away sat The Camper. The speaker divided his audience into groups of four. Each group was stationed by a large piece of paper hanging from the wall. Thomas, The Camper, and two young women were corralled into one group and told to make up some sort of list about something that they were supposed to share with the whole group. The two young women nodded as if they understood the object of the endeavor. Thomas did not really understand what the endeavor was, but did knw how to look as if he were intently involved. When it came to The Camper's turn to add something to the list, he very sweetly and calmly said that it takes time for him to sort things out and he wasn't ready. Thomas, surfacing from his own camouflaged confusion, stared at The Camper who introduced himself as John. He seemed so calm, not bored or defiant; he seemed like he wouldn't just play along for the sake of playing along; he had his own compass and map, maybe even his own presence. Yes, Thomas liked him or even more important Thomas was curious, and he hadn't been curious about anyone for years, those small hands: the young voice, but still such confidence, not the swaggering kind that begged for acclaim. How strange, how nice to see someone who…

Thomas' hands reached into the water. They swirled around as he was languidly search for prey. His hands stopped, resting beneath the waves.

The next day at the conference, Thomas followed the herd of benevolent attendees to the main dining hall; some sort of luncheon workshop. He walked between the tables covered in white linen; everyone seemed to find a pod in which to belong, everyone except Thomas. He walked nodding as casually as he could, smiling, embarrassed, looking for some pod into which he too could disappear. He watched the people chatting comfortably while they munched on their salads. They seemed to have some understanding with each other.

He noticed John looking as contented as a clam eating his salad, sitting by himself at a table. He seemed happy with his solitude. Thomas hovered there between the tables; he didn't want to appear forward and he definitely did not want to come across as a predatory shark. A very official and serious looking middle aged man stepped up to the podium in the center of the dining room. Thomas ducked down. Sidling between tables; he sat next to John.

John nodded at him, not unkindly, and continued to eat his salad. His frosty water glass was sweating on the white table cloth. Thomas's daring was wearing thin; his voice trembled. "How's the conference going? Your name is John isn't it?"

John looked up, surfacing from the depths of the salad bowl. He smiled. "All right."

Okay what should Thomas say next? "Some of the talks are pretty interesting."

"Some of them." John peered at Thomas as if looking for some sign. John didn't find it. He turned back to his salad.

After two solid days of being at the mercy of strangers, something snapped in Thomas. The speaker at the podium was droning on while words flashed on the Power Point screen. "Most of this really doesn't make sense to me. When I was young I learned to really try hard in school, but deep down I knew it didn't make sense."

John put his fork down and sat there absolutely still. He looked at Thomas. Whatever cue John had been waiting for, had occurred. "People pretend." He nodded confidentially to Thomas.

Thomas tried to shift his gaze away from John, but those eyes seemed, not exactly friendly, that's easy to counterfeit, but interested, interested deep down in some sort of strange way. Thomas struggled to maintain eye contact, swallowing slightly. The words just started to spill out. "Strange isn't it."

There was a moment of silent communion. The earnest voice of the lecturer seemed to evaporate: Power Point, a forgotten dream. John said, "It's a crazy world out there."

Thomas nodded in relief. He slowly scratched his head. "No matter how hard I try, eventually I blow it."

John watched, listening like a baby; that funny gaze, taking everything in without judgment. "You're lucky. You could have got stuck in pretending."

Thomas looked bewildered for a moment; slowly a smile dawned. "I suppose you're right."

And off they went balancing on a crazy edge, preposterously simple, not like falling in love, more like coming home. Thomas felt the cooling dishwater around his hands. He lifted his hands out of the water and for no good reason flicked his fingers into the air leaving behind a fine spray of bubbles that sparkled in the light of the overhead fixture. Not a rainbow exactly, but he smiled anyway.

John said that he was trans-gendered; certainly something for Thomas to ponder.

"Something to ponder," his voiced whispered on its own. Thomas slowly walked to his favorite place of pondering, through the dark dining room and into the even darker living room, he sat by the hummingbird lamp. His hand automatically switched it on. The humming birds sprung into existence as they circled the lamp, true, they were motionless, but definitely vivid. Thomas's face began staring out at those humming birds; he wondered if he was in love with John, although he couldn't imagine what they would do. And then even that didn't matter. There must be a kingdom of God somewhere in which all sorts of people can have implausible relationships, perhaps a realm of the imagination.

By the way John wondered if Thomas was trans-gendered too. Thomas pondered this new possibility. As a child, he had tried so hard to do what was right. Thomas shook his head slightly; not exactly what was right, but what people expected. Thomas lived in two different worlds: the world of necessity which seemed tight, anxious, and finally pointless, but which desperately needed to be maintained; and then there was that other world of fantastic dreams, dreams that needed to be hidden, more solemn than secrets, pearls beyond price to be stashed away so deeply that even he couldn't find them sometimes. Thomas frowned intensely; he admired the hummingbirds' silence, although finally they weren't very helpful.

On one side was Thomas, the boy becoming an old man, but who or what was on the other side, buried beyond the yearning, hidden melody? He glanced at the hummingbirds again, out of the corner of his eye in hopes of catching a sly movement or even twitch, the same way he used to secretly look at handsome men. Was that it? Just some secret appetite? There was the time in kindergarten when he told his friend, a girl (his friends were all girls back then) that he really would much rather play with dolls than footballs.

She looked very alarmed and serious the way young girls can before they start trying to please boys. She whispered in his ear, "You can never tell anybody about this. You must try to be a boy." She didn't talk much to Thomas after that. Once in a while when he would catch her staring him, he knew he needed to try harder. Thomas pondered that. A sly smile crept across his face. Now, she didn't actually say he should be a boy, but only that he should try to be one. But if he was only trying to be a boy, what was he?

Under the illumination of the lamp, Thomas cocked his head as if trying to hear some far off melody perhaps from the realm of the imagination. As the years went by, Thomas tried very hard to act like a boy, but like so many things in his life, it seemed to be a very difficult and frustrating task. In his early twenties he learned about being gay and found what solace he could. But with all the men he loved, there was something inside of himself that wasn't true. He was still trying.

Thomas watched the lamp. His face relaxed, only his deep breathing betrayed any kind of excitement, some new, actually some old idea dawning. He stood up. This time, with a sense of purpose he walked out of the room.

What about Danny? Thomas wondered. Danny was charming and impulsive, but appeared to have no deep awareness of his own motives. Danny just went ahead and did things. It didn't faze him that he was on his fifth job in five years and that with heart disease and diabetes he still lived the high life. But Danny persistently demonstrated a kind of devotedness to his loved ones, even when he criticized them. Thomas wondered if he had ever been devoted to anybody... maybe Joe, but finally that didn't count.

And Danny truly was devoted to Thomas in that mysterious way of his. Of course Danny believed that angels were watching over him. All and all, Danny's life seemed more...not real exactly, maybe just less constrained than Thomas'.

He heard the television switch on in the bedroom. He surfaced out of the pool of his imagination and walked into the bedroom and sat on the edge of the bed next to Danny's form. "Hi honey, there's something I want to talk with you about."

Danny's face stared intently at the television screen. THE WHEEL OF FORTUNE flashing, reverberating through the room.

Thomas took a deep breath.

Danny glanced away from the television screen. "What's up?" The sound of clapping coming from the screen drew his attention back to the screen.

"I've been thinking about something. You know John who I talked about from San Francisco; he's transgender, female to male."

Danny's interest was sparked. "Has he had the operation? Does he have the equipment yet?"

Thomas looked bewildered for an instant. "I don't know. He frowned, "It's not important."

"Sure is important to somebody."

Thomas' usually hooded eyes opened and sparked. He turned away from Danny. "That stuff is only a little part of sexuality; it's who you are inside that matter."

Danny looked back at the television.

"I've been thinking about myself."

Danny turned, eyeing Thomas cautiously.

The fire in Thomas' eyes had dampened slightly.

Danny was caught between trying to listen to Thomas and his television show.

Thomas looked solemnly at Danny's face. "Inside it feels like I'm a girl. When I look back, it's the way it's always been. I had this dream and I think I understand what it was telling me, showing me."

Danny fixed his sights on Thomas. "You'll change your mind next week like you always do." He turned back to the television.

Thomas looked deep in thought again. "I don't know about that. I do know that I want to be able to grow up. I had this dream about a girl. I killed her, but she is coming back now. At first it seemed like a nightmare. Then I let go; I felt this happiness. Inside I'm a girl, truly, truly. Maybe I can grow."

Danny's attention focused on his partner. "I found a round trip fare to Phoenix for $150." WHEEL OF FORTUNE pulled his face back to the television screen.

Thomas studied the back of Danny's head. She knew Danny took things in, in a strange way, sort of nonchalantly, but deeper than he first showed

Chapter 4

··

Thomas sat by the dining room table; she gingerly picked up the phone receiver and slowly pressed in the numbers. She tried to sound as cheery as possible. "Presence, hi how are you?"

There was a long pause drenched in significance. "It's been raining all day. Can't you hear?" The faint tapping of rain on a metal rooftop filtered across two thousand miles.

For a moment Thomas was lost in the mystery; strange, being in two places at once. She shook her head; it's important to be sympathetic. She snapped to attention. "That's too bad, what a bummer."

A waterlogged voice said feebly, "How are things there?

"You know; cold and dark."

They commiserated with each other in silence.

Thomas began clicking her heels together softly. She

took a deep breath, eyes wide in anticipation. "Danny found a really cheap fare to Phoenix. It's all set. I talked with Joe and you can park in his driveway and use the shower."

There was a dangerously long silence.

Thomas held her breath.

"Did you buy the ticket yet?" Presence's voice wavered in embarrassment, an emotion usually not part of her repertoire.

Thomas looked panicked. Her lips mouthed words but nothing came out except, "Ah…"

Presence's words interrupted that wavering note. Once again her voice spoke in a staccato rhythm. "I can't make it all the way to Tucson. I'm going to a retreat in San Jose and I'll never make it on time…can you get your ticket refunded?"

The panicked look on Thomas's face released; she was staring into the infinite again.

"Say something."

"I don't know."

"What kind of answer is that? Did you buy it?"

"I did." She looked down mumbling and finally took a deep breath; her neck straightened as she looked out into the darkness of the window. "I did."

Another long pause as they both listened to the sound of rain in the state of Washington. The edge of Presence's voice was softening. "I didn't think…" Her voice resumed its customary pace. "I'm meeting the Plumber's family after Christmas. I can't make it to Tucson."

Thomas looked like she was seeing something faintly peering back at her from the window. The edges of her mouth twitched slightly. "It's okay." Yes, her eyes had definitely noticed something. "I haven't seen Joe for a long time anyway." Animation flickered in her face. Yes, an adventure, she and Joe used to go on adventures, even if Thomas had to be tricked into going.

She heard the television click off in the other room. Danny's footsteps approached; Thomas hooded her eyes.

"Do you want to go to the Wilde Roast and look at the gay boys?" Danny smiled with the enticing supplication.

Thomas glanced up, eyes still hooded. "Oh I think I'll just hang out. I have some papers I need to grade."

For an instant Danny's face shifted through disappointment, then irritation and finally to sly excitement. "I'll be back later." He grabbed his coat.

"Presence called..." Thomas' voice was left hanging in the air.

Danny paused. "The elusive Presence, what's up with her now?"

Thomas eyes hooded even more. "She says she can't make it to Tucson."

"It's that guy, isn't it?"

"No...sort of" Thomas glanced away.

"When is she going to grow up?"

Something fired in Thomas. "Since when do you know so much about growing up?"

They faced off.

Danny shrugged and headed toward the door, his mind on his adventure.

Thomas watched him. "I'll be okay, just fine…you have a good time."

Danny disappeared through the door.

Thomas settled into a corner of the sofa, her mind peopled with ghosts, memories of friends and lovers from long ago. Their distance in time and space made them safe guests. She jerked her head slightly as if she were shaking something off and picked up a book from a stack on the coffee table. She held it solemnly with both hands. Then she opened the cover watching the ghosts fly out from the open pages. Lately she had been reading biographies, Benjamin Franklin, Anais Nin, Carl Jung, Mae West, Louis Armstrong, Eleanor Roosevelt, Maya Angelou; she was so curious how other people actually set up their lives and then, how they coped with what happened to them. She could sit for hours entranced, possessed by ghosts struggling to clarify the mystery of their lives. Every once in a while she would secretly glance at the humming birds.

She opened a biography of Henry Miller. After all if Danny could live on the wild side, Thomas could too. Just as she was settling into reading about Henry and springtime in Paris, the sound of the porch screen door opening pulled rudely her back to winter in Minneapolis. She froze in absolute stillness, hoping that she would be camouflaged by the inanimate objects around her. The footsteps continued across the porch. They stopped by front of the door, a moment of silence, then the sound of gentle tapping; her camouflage didn't work. Frowning she looked up from her book and turned toward the door, rubbing the ghosts out of her eyes. Through the door window she made out a form, long brownish curly hair; an elongated neck on which a head perched proudly, large woman features, a face fierce and pleading at the same time: Rose Marie.

With some effort, tentatively smiling; Thomas pushed up from the sofa. She swung the door open; Rose Marie stood there framed. Thomas paused for an instant, uncertain what to do with a living person.

Though her face was still, Rose Marie's eyes seemed to vibrate with both need and defiance, a mistress of metamorphosis.

"Hi Rose Marie, how ya doing?" Thomas slipped into her folksiest smile.

"Am I bothering you?" Her voice sound sounded meek, but she defiantly took off her coat and threw it on a chair. Long dangerous earrings glittered from her poised head and dangled down almost touching her frilly girlish blouse.

Thomas watched the flickering metamorphoses. "Come on in; good to see you."

The pleading girl won out. Rose Marie slumped into the room as if she had just run away from home. "I thought that you might want to go for a walk."

Thomas pondered the question. She had been with so many ghosts lately that it took her a moment to actually figure out if this was a flesh and blood question. She could tell by her anxious pulse that this wasn't a phantom whimsy, but a real human bodied request, fueled by some kind of pulsing need. She glanced toward a window and the frigid darkness beyond it. "It's pretty cold."

The pleading look on Rose Marie's her face began deflating into disappointment.

Maybe if Thomas pretended that Rose Marie was a ghost. "You know it's so...dark."

Rose Marie's body straightened, a stubborn defiance freezing her eyes. "Well if you don't want to..." Her voice sounded like an open wound.

Thomas nodded, yes, Rose Marie was most definitely a living person, ghosts don't have definite needs. Thomas took a deep breath. "Why don't you come in and sit down. I'll make a cup of tea." She smiled reassuringly.

Rose Marie paused for an instant, as if she didn't quite remember who she was.

Thomas, like a dutiful chamberlain, waved her arm majestically toward the sofa.

Rose Marie smiled gratefully and settled into the sofa: a girl found.

Thomas needed time to take in the warm urgent mystery of it all. "Give me a minute; I'll put some water on." After giving Rose Marie the most gracious smile that Thomas could muster, she sailed into the kitchen sanctuary, faucets and pans and cups, preparing her for the world of people.

As she poured the steaming water into the cups, she glanced at herself in the darkened kitchen window; she looked at the reflection of the old Thomas, the familiar *he.* Then the *she* stared at each other. They studied each other curiously, then both smiled in a kind if truce. Together they both poured the steaming water into the teapots. Thomas turned away from the image and once again was the newly christened singular *she.*

Holding two warm steaming cups she joined Rose Marie on the sofa. They sat there silently, both curled up and enveloped by the soft padding. Thomas looked at her from her corner. "How's your day Rose Marie?"

She frowned. "Today…today's all right."

Thomas nodded as sagely.

" I kept busy." She shook her head. "Yesterday I didn't get up until noon."

"Did that company ever call back after your second interview?"

Sarah looked at Thomas with raw disappointment and then looked away into space.

"I'm sorry."

Once again Rose Marie's face was a battlefield, an angry woman and lost girl in combat. Then her face took on that strange blank look of someone who forgot for an instant where she was or why she had come to this place, or even who she was; she sank deeper into the sofa. From somewhere in its padded depths a voice issued forth. "I'm tired of talking about all that. How are you doing?"

Thomas responded to the disembodied voice. "Are you sure?"

"I want to hear about somebody else." Her voice sounded definite,

Casually almost cheerfully Thomas addressed the sofa. "Well I'm still reading biographies, school's kind of interesting when I don't feel like I'm a phony, Danny and I are doing okay, I'm going to Tucson on Saturday, and did I mention to you that I'm a woman now?"

Rose Marie's body jolted.

"It's not really a big deal."

"Not a big deal?" She perched on the edge of the sofa examining Thomas.

It was Thomas' turn to sink into the sofa.

Rose Marie shook her head formidably. "But you're a man!"

Thomas squirmed around in the sofa for a few moments. An apprentice sorcerer that Thomas was becoming, spoke up. "I know I have a man's body, but inside I'm a girl. I didn't even quite realize it. I knew there was something that didn't fit. Isn't that funny?"

Rose Marie's face looked blank as gears began shifting.

" I didn't have any way to grow up, I was too busy trying to be a boy, and at 59 that's a...a problem."

Rose Marie's eyes roamed across the map of Thomas' features looking for familiar landmarks.

"You see..." Thomas' voice trailed off into cold stubbornness.

"You're a handsome man." Rose Marie protested weakly.

Thomas turned away.

"But what about how you look?"

Thomas' body, slumped into the sofa, then stirred,

uncoiling. Her eyes focused on Rose Marie's face; Thomas didn't look folksy anymore. "I don't care how I look. I just want to be able to grow up. This is it for me."

Transfixed in each other's eyes, neither could escape.

A growing relief began filtering into Rose Marie's face as if she had finally recognized a familiar landmark. She studied the backed-against-the-wall defiance in her friend's face. She smiled.

Thomas took a deep breath of relief.

She winked at Thomas. "Well girlfriend, do you want to go shopping?"

Thomas looked startled, touching her face tentatively. She frowned, stubbornness reemerging. "I want to be a woman, not just a girl."

The expression of Rose Marie's face remained steady.

Thomas' wariness began dissipating.

Rose Marie smiled gently. "You see that's not how it works exactly. The girl grows into the woman. You have to be a girl first."

Wide eyed, Thomas listened.

Chapter 5

A dark Saturday morning...Thomas woke up, glancing at the glowing numbers on the clock...a few more minutes to sleep. Danny lay softly snoring; he didn't need to get up until right before they drove to the airport. Digital clocks are so silent, no ticking to camouflage the mystery of time, no hands moving to force the present in some sort of mechanical direction, just numbers appearing silently, like the painted humming birds; they never really move, or if they did it was in secret; he glanced over at Danny listening to his breaths marking a pathway of time; maybe that's why people get married: those breaths. She frowned; why was she going on this trip anyway? She turned onto her back, just another frightening inconvenience breaking a routine that was already fraught with peril.

As if in a play that someone else had written, in which she was reluctantly performing, she mechanically sat up. Moving to the steady beat of Danny's breathing, Thomas's ghostly shape edged out of bed. Her shadow tiptoed across the floor and reached toward a dark pile lying there. The two shadowy shapes merged and tiptoed over to the dark shape of the bed. The three shadows merged. The bed springs trembled, tittering in surprise at the mass of the insubstantial shadows.

She sat there on the edge of the bed, easing into being a person, a person about to take a trip, about to drop off the edge of a cliff with no bottom in sight. She glanced at the glowing digital clock face; she had time.

Sitting there, she nestled into her memories; she always woke up minutes and sometimes hours before the horrible jolt of an alarm. There was some feeble protection in anticipating danger even if that anticipation left her tired and frazzled the next day. She liked to be prepared as she was pulled into the void, pulled by some dark singularity whose mass was so immense that it had been silently secretly drawing her into its dark maw her entire life. She had prepared her clothing last night as if she would actually be doing something with them other than slipping into the void. Somewhere in that void was Tucson. She pulled on her socks the warmth felt good, even on the disappearing edge of the universe, she could still feel comfort...comfort...she needed to dress warmly enough to get to the airport in frigid Minneapolis, but still not too warmly for sunny Tucson. This was a particular challenge since she would only be taking a knapsack; she traveled light as she straddled worlds.

In the bedroom the winter morning light reluctantly

began turning shadows into three dimensional forms. She stared at the dark lump of a knapsack leaning against the bureau. With rapt concentration she kept exchanging piles of clothes between the bureau and the knapsack to the sound of Danny's deep sleep breathing. She finally closed the bureau drawer with doomsday resignation. Her face frozen into a solemn mask as if she were preparing for some inevitable and mysterious sacrament. She knew she was forgetting something, something vital; of course that is how she always felt. There, sitting nondescript on the bureau was a worn copy of *Pride and Prejudice.* She picked it up tenderly and placed it next to her bulging knapsack.

Thomas sat down slowly on the bed; the clock face had mysteriously changed. She took a deep breath, bent over and reached for her pants; the bed trembled like some living creature. Oblivious to the stirring life beneath it, Danny's breath continued at its regular pace. With an approximation of resolve Thomas pulled her trousers over her ankles, pulled socks up to her ankles, slipped into shoes somewhere below her ankles and then awkwardly tied up the loose ends of shoe laces. She thrust herself upward into the shadowy room and pulled up her trousers. She stood still for a moment hardly believing her metamorphosis. The trip was beginning. In the faint light of a cold morning, she slung the knapsack over her shoulder and walked into the living room. She stared out the window, light just beginning to turn an unpromising shade of gray. Naively, as if the world weren't ending, her neighbor casually walked out of her house leading her dog.

Thomas softly stepped back into the bedroom, watched Danny breathing for a moment and then brushed his cheek with her lips. "Time to get up, honey."

Danny rolled on his back, cracking his eyelids open and puckering his lips to make a lazy kissing sound.

"It's time darling; whatever that is." Thomas turned on the bedside lamp and nostalgically watched Danny groggily sit up wiping his dreams from his eyes: gray haired boy. Thomas tore herself away from that bubble of sentiment and hurried into her sanctuary, the kitchen, to that place where she did reassuring things. The deck window facing east brightening…was that a little color on the horizon? She had her usual breakfast to make and her usual rituals to accomplish: stretching her body, brushing her teeth, combing her thinning hair in the mirror while trying to ignore the haunted image looking back at her. Her body gradually took on life, a stuff so vulnerable to accident.

By the time Danny and Thomas stepped out of the house, it was a winter morning, sky just beginning to turn a cool northern color, almost blue…not hopeful exactly but tender. Danny, the high priest, led Thomas into the mystery. Thomas solemnly followed his lead. The car roared and took off, Thomas staring out the window in a daze…good day to die. The car sped through the quiet Saturday morning streets and finally reached the hub of the airport, cars eternally driving around and up to the huge smashingly bright bastion of change.

Danny turned the car down a dark passageway. The darkness slowly transformed into a ghostly lit indoor parking lot, a quiet anteroom. Their footsteps echoed between the endless haunted rows of silent cars.

Danny pushed a glass door open; Thomas followed before the door shut. She stepped into the bright bubble of the airport. A different kind of quietness reigned, a quietness humming with whispers. People waited in long lines speaking in hushed solemn voices as if they were in church. Though they were dressed in gaudy holiday costumes they moved solemnly towards the mysterious sacrament, pushing their baggage closer and closer to the altar where they would receive their permission for passage, hoping that they wouldn't be the bloody sacrifice. Danny scoped out the terrain and led the way toward a line. Thomas hung back, knapsack on her back and a book in her hand. Danny stopped abruptly at the end of the line and turned around to Thomas who increased her speed to stand next to him.

Danny looked concerned. "Now you've got your ID?"

For an instant Thomas looked blank.

Danny's concern turned into impatience. "You need that...not many people would let their spouses spend a week alone with an old boyfriend."

Thomas fumbled through her wallet, little slips of paper raining down on the ground. She pulled out her drivers' license, a look of relief on her face. "I've got it."

Danny stared at the little slips of paper on the floor.

Thomas noticed the pile and bent down, knapsack

and all. "It's been twenty years, and Joe and I really have finished things."

Danny looked doubtful.

"You're wonderful to be so kind to me, dropping me off and all. How could I not love you?" Danny looked a little flustered but pleased. "I'm begging for compliments again."

"You deserve it."

The two paused as they talked; the line in front of them kept moving, drawn through a flimsy arch around which guards fighting boredom had stationed themselves. With an urgent nod of his head, Danny motioned Thomas to move up. Danny said, "You don't need to check in. I think you're all set."

Thomas breathing rapidly kept glancing toward the arch which seemed to be swallowing the line of people in front of him. "That's good," she said feebly.

Danny studied his partner skeptically and touched her shoulder.

Thomas moved closer to Danny.

Danny flashed a reassuring smile. "Don't pick up any strange men."

Thomas smiled a dooms day smile and pressed herself against Danny.

Danny nodded toward the line which was leaving the two behind.

Thomas scrambled into place, her chest contained by the straps of the knapsack, expanding and contracting in rapid breaths. Her feet moved forward at a steady determined pace as she glanced up at the front of the line, right by the arch, where people were taking off their shoes and then piling the shoes, wallets, purses and whatever was in their pockets into open bins that they would then set on a conveyor belt. With contained terror people watched those bins loaded with the precious mementos of their lives move along the conveyor belt and disappear through rubber flaps into darkness. With desperate faith they watched the treasures of their lives disappear as they stepped through the sacred arch and into the space between here and there. Occasionally the arch emitted a sharp blaring sound. The line of people would freeze, everyone watching passively as guards would single someone out for scrutiny. When the buzzing would stop, people looked relieved and continued to process under The Arch of Judgment. Thomas' feet moved forward toward the spectacle that would soon engulf her. Were they headed toward salvation or to death?

Danny, a stationary island, watched Thomas move forward.

Thomas, like Lots wife, stopped and looked back.

A woman behind him pushed her suite case against Thomas' shoe. Her body cringed.

Danny urgently waved Thomas forward.

Thomas focused on Danny. She smiled gratefully at him and turned around toward the object poking her. "Oh I'm sorry. I get spacey sometimes when I travel."

The insistent young woman gave the slightest hint of a nod and turned away.

Thomas approached The Arch of Judgment. She

paused, a hopeless look on her face knowing that any judgment would find her wanting. Grimly she bent over and began undoing her shoelaces…meeting judgment without shoes, she shook her head and with resignation slipped off her shoes. They hung from her hands like dead animals. The person in front of her reluctantly placed his last possessions in the bin and moved solemnly toward The Arch. A good day to die… it's time…with methodical speed Thomas started divesting herself of her intimate possessions. Her knapsack, PRIDE AND PREJUDICE with her ticket between its pages, and the rest of her meager life lying nestled in the bin. Hesitantly she set the bin onto the moving conveyor belt. The floor felt cool beneath her feet as the bin disappeared into the veiled darkness. When one doesn't actually believe in time, letting go of things can be very mysterious.

Now it was her turn to enter under the magic arch… is she a sheep or a goat …she knew the answer already. She peered through The Arch at the Promised Land from which she knew he would be forbidden by an edgy god. On the other side The Saved, embarrassed, were putting their shoes on and grabbing their wallets and purses. There…she put her foot through…silence… her whole body crossed the threshold…no alarm; she evaded judgment…a temporary fluke…she would have a future for a while at least. The bin carrying her intimate possessions popped through the veiled box. The sight of her scuffed shoes brought her back to the present, or was it the future? She turned around peering through

The Arch at that other world that held Danny…Danny standing there disconsolately looking into space.

Danny feeling Thomas' gaze turned towards The Arch.

Their eyes connected creating a present moment. Thomas smiled with stiff resolution. Danny nodded valiantly toward The Path that Thomas faced. Another bin popped through the veiled box; suddenly aware of her nakedness, Thomas balancing on one foot, tottered, scrambling to put her shoe on. She sheepishly fished after the keys and coins in the bin then grabbed onto her book for dear life. Once again she turned and peered through what seemed miles and miles of space and time looking for Danny.

Danny's face, soft and lonely and old hung in the distance like some moon of memory.

Thomas waved bravely to get his attention.

Danny half smiled and waved back. His body turned away to the present of his life in which Thomas would be a ghost.

Thomas mouthed, "I love you" to know one in particular.

Chapter 5

The stewardess shut the door sealing the passengers into the plane. There was the slightest moment of silence, the hardly noticeable solemnity of fear as passengers entered the gap between one place and another. Even time flickered as they began preparing to change time zones. Thomas stared at the faces around him, faces that during one strange moment in the air would actually grow one hour younger.

The sound of a baby fussing triggered the hum of conversation and life as usual...as usual...time curling up cozily on a rainy afternoon with nothing special to do, stretching out in the comfortable promise of sameness. But Thomas knew this comfort wasn't the present; in the present anything could, would happen: earthquakes, the flu, falling in love, plane crashes; anything. Even as the rest of the passengers were trying to settle into strained coziness, Thomas was breathing, shallow and fast, her eyes focused intensely on the words marching across the page of the open book on her lap, "It is a truth universally acknowledged that a single man in possession of a good fortune must be in want of a wife." The engines of the plane roared; the plane jolted slightly and began backing up slowly, separating from the dock. Ghostly explosions burst behind her eyeballs. She riveted her attention to her book. "However little known the feelings or views of such a man may be on first entering a neighborhood, this truth is so well fixed…" Out of the corner of her eye she could see, slowly sailing by, trucks and bundled up airport attendants doing their ordinary tasks as if nothing were ever going to happen.

The plane paused, waiting for something. Then suddenly as unexpectedly as the digital numbers on a clock face change, the plane accelerated. Her hands gripped her book; she couldn't help but watch the landscape of the airport rushing faster and faster across the window. The roaring grew louder and she could feel the deep shudder of the plane straining to a breaking point. Just when she was sure the plane would blow apart, implausibly it started pointing upwards. Her hands pressing together as if in prayer, closing the book; she desperately waited for the tail of the plane to scrap against the ground splitting the craft open. One final deafening roar, her face turned directly toward the blue window; the craft shot up as smoothly as a knife cutting through soft blue butter. She felt her hands and her feet and face relax in this escape from death. Her eyes softened; she was alive and speeding smoothly upward into the buoyant blue, blue, blue purring all around her and stretching into her imagination.

In a bubble of temporary safety she took in the routine sounds in the cabin: voices talking, still hushed, the constrained roar of the engine and a baby's cries. She noticed the man sitting next to her, a flushed beefy face, hands slightly puffy but strong with a showy diamond ring on the pinky figure of his left hand.

As if on cue the man turned to him. "You from Arizona?" He looked at Thomas with friendly directness.

"Oh no, I'm just going to visit a friend in Tucson… for a few days."

"Lotsa rain this year."

"Ya?" Thomas decided that she liked her companion.

"Haven't had much rain for seven years and now it's raining every day."

"Yikes!" Thomas looked impressed.

Her companion reassured her. "Won't be bad though, at least compared to Minneapolis."

Thomas looked duly reassured. "Where are you from?"

"Tempe, My wife and me have a place there. I'm coming back from a pilots' convention in New York."

"Do you fly planes?" Wide-eyed Thomas looked at the pilot.

"Got one back home, been doing it for years." His diamond ring glinted in the light streaming through the window.

Thomas tightened a little, afraid of being a pest. She glanced at her book for reassurance, but her companion smiled with the pleasure of someone setting out into a story.

Thomas smiled back; she loved to hear people talk about themselves.

"Yup, been doing it for years. I have me a little company back home. Great country; if you work hard, you can get anything you want. At least that's what I tell my kids." He gave Thomas a half wink. "They're not kids anymore but you know what I mean."

Thomas's face tightened slightly; she had a vague suspicion of anything that sounded too matter of fact, especially since she really didn't believe in time. She noticed the wedding ring on the Pilot's finger. "I suppose so, but sometimes things aren't that simple."

Her companion frowned in bewilderment, and there was a moment of silence like when the door of the plane was shut. The Pilot shook his head with a little jerk. "Seems some people just try to get in the way and don't listen, like in politics."

Thomas looked thoughtfully at The Pilot, "Those television sound bites seem pretty silly."

Her companion looked reassured. "Those democrats don't listen to sense. We need to get back to real values again. Do you remember the fifties?"

"Sure..."

"Well people knew about politeness and hard work." He nodded expectantly at Thomas.

Thomas looked down for just an instant and then glanced at her companion. "Oh," there was a long doubtful pause. "I know things seemed pretty orderly when I was a kid in St. Paul, but I remember on the news seeing dogs being sent on black children. Maybe things only looked pretty good if you were..." He paused at loss for a word, "comfortable."

The Pilot jerked his head slightly as if he were shaking off a fly. All the time though he kept smiling urgently. "There's always something not quite right, but it was the values we all had."

Thomas nodded slightly then stared out into space as if she were watching the humming birds on the lamp. There, she caught the briefest of flickers, her face brightened. "I do remember how everybody I knew as a kid seemed to believe a lot of the same things." He paused again. "But for me I was a little homosexual kid, and there was no place for me other than being sick or bad. I like some difference, it gives people a chance." She looked with innocent satisfaction at his companion.

The Pilot looked way, his body tensing.

Thomas glanced back at the book on her lap.

Her companion turned back with insistent resolve. "People worked together."

Thomas looked up from his book. She looked at the pilot's face as if searching for a flicker of understanding. "I like when people work together, and I do think we are losing that, but difference is really important. Difference can help people work together when they..." She was at a loss for words again. The she smiled. "They can be creative even when it gets messy."

Her companion's face softened slightly as if the possibility of a reconciliation were stirring somewhere within him, a real but fitful event certainly far short of approval. "One of my nephews is a gay, and I told him, that's okay. I told him that that's his own business, but I don't want to hear anything about marriage."

Thomas looked startled for a second and then began piecing the words together. "I can see why you think that with religion and all, but when my partner goes to the hospital or when we try to own things together, the law makes it hard on us, as if it doesn't recognize that we are building a life together. We're..." She frowned searching for a word; she was really crunching. "... disappeared."

That face that had intrepidly piloted planes across darkened obscure skies without ever losing its bearing flickered in doubt. "I'd just like everybody to be happy as they can."

"Me too." Thomas, an expert on watching, noticed the flicker; she smiled with secret excitement and knew it was time to stop. She looked into The Pilot's eyes with the innocence of a devious child. "Does it every get scary when you fly a plane?"

The Pilot intrepidly looked out into the distance. "I used to be a pilot in Alaska before we had all those instruments..."

Thomas settled into listening to The Pilot's stories, barely interrupted by the stewardess passing out pretzels and beverages. The last story finally sputtered out when there was a subtle shift of the plane as it began its very first descent to Phoenix. As Thomas turned her attention to the window, she saw the ground far below slowly rising up until she could see beetles scurrying along the thin ribbons of road. Perhaps it was the presence of The Pilot by her side, Thomas wasn't afraid, just curious.

The Pilot began talking to the man behind him about the stock market. Whatever the Pilot and Thomas had shared evaporated as the plane approached its planned destination. The plane began its curving, tilted descent to the airport. The sun shone into the window like a miraculous inspiration and then passed. Those were cars not beetles...the ground pushed its way up to the plane. The wheels rubbed against the ground in a rough kiss; the engine blasted in climactic triumph as the plane slowed down, and Phoenix airport glided across the windows.

The passengers stirred restlessly and finally got up before the plane came to its predictable stop. The Pilot stood up matter-of-factly still talking to passenger behind him. Whatever contact he had with Thomas seemed to disappear in the bustle of opening overhead compartments.

Thomas glanced at her companion a few times, but The Pilot seemed totally absorbed in his conversation with the man behind. The Pilot eagerly pushed away from his seat as if there were something chasing him. Thomas sat there like a ghost...how strange to suddenly to be disappeared. A little smile edged across her face as she watched the passengers anxiously bustle; there is a sense of privacy in invisibility. The chaos within the cabin was slowly being channeled into a pattern as rows of passengers began systematically emptying into the aisle.

Thomas slowly stood up and joined her row as it emptied into the aisle. She was standing right behind The Pilot. Thomas sped forward and peeked her head over his shoulder. "Nice to meet you."

The Pilot glanced up quickly and nodded at Thomas without making eye contact.

Thomas watched with a funny little smile on her face… so much for the Fifties.

The slowly moving river of passengers was now being evacuated in peristaltic waves through the open door of the plane. Just before Thomas was pushed out the plane, she had to make it through the gauntlet of smiling stewardess and stewards, each thrusting a nodding smile at the passengers who were already metamorphosing into possible future customers. Then she found herself with other murmuring passengers now processing through a purgatorial, shadowy tube that hopefully exited into the bliss of the terminal. Thomas didn't trust the possibility of heaven much; she looked down at her feet rhythmically stepping up the rubberized floor, so far so good. The light of paradise unexpectedly flooded around her, she entered the Light of the terminal.

She had never really considered what she would do if against all odds she walked through those pearly gates. She stood still, amazed and even alarmed; her face tightened, her eyes searching for some sort of direction. She shoved her hand ferociously into her right pants' pocket and pulled out a small piece of paper. Flashing a relieved grin at no one in particular, she opened the folded treasure map and studied it intently. She nodded her head as she read the instructions, her lips mouthing words. Joe had been very specific about things: first she needed to find the bus; there would be a sign. Then take the bus to the last stop and finally she needed to call Richard who would pick her up if Joe hadn't arrived home yet.

Thomas stared at the little piece of paper with sentences scribbled on it, her hand clenching it. A visit to Joe's world would begin; Joe always lived at the hub of things, not that he was outgoing or even wanted that central position; people, especially men, positioned themselves around him. What was it about him? He was attractive, but there were other attractive men who didn't get all that attention. He didn't hold court the way Danny did, but people just wanted to be around Joe, Joe, a strange mixture of innocence, self-destructiveness, kindness, obliviousness. There was always something hidden about him, yes, it was the hiddenness that drew people, some secret peeking out of his brown eyes, with each blink those eyes inviting and then withholding, with each blink the secret becoming more tantalizing. Thomas' hand closed, crumbling the piece of paper. She looked up; yes, the Phoenix airport and things to be done.

Thomas, knapsack on her back, delicately folded the little slip of paper into a small packet and pushed it into her pocket then tucked the battered copy of

Pride and Prejudice in her other pocket. Faced with confusion, she usually started any challenge by asking questions, lots of questions. When she was younger and had the appeal of youthful innocence, people, often complete strangers, ushered her towards her goals. Now as a graying older person, people tended to avoid her, not consciously perhaps, but never the less. She tugged reassuring at the shoulder straps of his knapsack. She WOULD find her destination. By the third stranger that she questioned, she spotted the bus ticket counter in the distance. Zoning in on it, her feet pushed on. A wave of satisfaction, not salvation, flooded through her…salvation…she wondered…in a world spinning in a cosmos not measured by time, perhaps temporary destinations were as good as it gets. She stepped up to the bus counter.

There, plastered on the wall above a very imposing desk, names of cities and towns…yes, there it is…"TUCSON" was printed in large black print. Underneath the names of so many destinations, a Black Woman reigned with imposing majesty. She sat behind that desk checking little pieces of paper with cool nonchalance. Occasionally she would pick up one piece, glance at it suspiciously and finally very emphatically place it aside. Thomas watched as power smoldered under the surface of that emphatic gesture. Finally unable to contain herself any longer, she rested her hand softly on the counter. "I'm going to Tucson…please?"

Her Majesty glanced up for an instant only to return

to her pieces of paper. "That's what it says." Clearly she was a woman of few words.

Thomas stood there nodding. "It does, doesn't it? Right there." She even pointed to the sign.

Her Majesty glowered at an offending piece of paper and moved it aside. "Now that we've got that settled…" Her voice droned out into nothing.

Thomas nodded. "I want to get to Tucson as soon as possible."

Her Majesty studied Thomas blankly. "That'll be $27.50 please." Her fingers nonchalantly tapped something out on the cash register; a little tab of paper slowly pushed its way out of the machine.

Thomas watched her magic trick.

Her Majesty handed Thomas a piece of paper, looking at her for the first time.

Trapped under her gaze Thomas looked blank for an instant. "Ya." She mumbled to no one in particular, her hand scrambling into her pocket again, pulling out a beat up old wallet and studying the contents with anxious gravity.

As Her Majesty's fingers drummed on the desk, her eyes studied Thomas with the detached irony of a goddess…not exactly benevolent, but certainly all knowing.

Thomas picked out the precious bills. "Five…ten… fifteen…twenty five." She stuck her other hand in her other pocket and pulled out a handful of change and deposited two quarters on the counter and looked up, a job well done. "There it is!"

Her Majesty didn't need to count the money out again. She gave Thomas a quick nod, the offering received, and then turned back to her pile of papers.

Thomas remained glued to the ground watching her expectantly.

She glanced up, surprised that Thomas was still in front of her. "Well?"

She looked befuddled. "Um, how...?" His voice disappeared into confusion.

She relented. "Anytime now...as soon as the van arrives."

"So I'll just..."

She looked at him with surprising sympathy. "I'll call you."

He looked at her anxiously.

"I won't let you miss it."

Thomas smiled, making eye contact with her and shuffled away stopping just far enough to be out of Her Majesty's vision and close enough so that she could keep her in view. Three other people were waiting, standing there like remote sentinels. Thomas took up her position. Occasionally she would glance up at the clock over the counter, look worried, and finally glance for reassurance at Her Majesty behind the counter. After all she was omnipotent and reigned somewhere beyond time.

Her Majesty looked up from the pile, glancing at the supplicants around her, and picked up the phone. She said something and then nodded with satisfaction. Putting her pen down, she looked at each of her charges and stepped out from her behind her desk. "Follow me."

Jesus couldn't have said it with more authority. And they followed her.

Thomas joined in the procession. Midway to the door to the outside a look of anxious doubt disturbed Thomas' peaceful devotion; her steps began slowing until they stopped all together. She took out her wallet and stared with concern at its contents. The rest of the procession was moving inexorably toward the door. The Her Majesty turned around; there was a hint of displeasure on her face. She fixed her eyes on Thomas. Thomas looked up; Her Majesty nodded. There… Thomas found her ticket. Stuffing the wallet back in her pocket she scrambled to the end of the line. She smiled with relief, a lost lamb, now found.

They marched out of the terminal and into the cool air full of the sounds of traffic. A white van stood at the curb ahead. Thomas could see the palm trees standing, guarding the busy street, vertical stripes framing the sky. The procession stopped by the van; a large man bulging out of a nondescript uniform appeared as if out of nowhere. Her Majesty nodded at her large attendant as he posted himself by the door of the van, calmly opening a side panel to reveal a cavernous space. Two supplicants, women, scurried from their places in the procession to be the first in line.

The attendant nodded at them. "Luggage to check?"

They both nodded back.

"Where to?" He grabbed their two suitcases.

In accidental harmony they said, "Valpariso," and stared at each other in surprise.

"You're going there too?" A tall plain looking woman with a tight face and dull straight hair glanced beseechingly at her newly found companion, a tall woman with a very red heart-shaped mouth, mirrored sun glasses, and glamorously curly hair. The Glamorous Woman looked with overblown charm at The Plain Woman. "How delightful."

Thomas studied the new-found friends…both women on the slippery edge of middle age, facing it without wedding rings.

He looked closer at the two. In the glare of daylight the Glamorous Woman's vivid makeup appeared powdery, a courageous attempt to cover fine wrinkles around her mouth and eyes. Now free of her burden, she placed her large soft hands on her hips and shot a dazzling smile at the Plain Woman.

The Plain Woman looked down shyly, and finally mustered enough courage to glance up at her glamorous companion. "Looks like we're getting off at the same stop. Have you ever been there before?"

The Glamorous Woman looked at the Plain Woman with sparkling confidence. "It's the last stop before Tucson. Tucson's a great city, everything you want." She led the way into the van with the other woman in tow.

Thomas watched them intently.

A voice broke her attention. "Baggage?"

Thomas startled. "Ugh…oh no." She nodded as kindly as she could to that insistent face, and then followed the two women. Something about their eyes touched him, age peeking out, that funny kind of fear of becoming older women who have never been married, no place in the world, ghosts She followed them into the van, sitting just behind them.

The two spoke softly.

Thomas sat down...better buckle herself in too. Her eyes searched the van. Finally she discovered the seat belt receptacle, but where's the belt? She frowned, containing her panic; she knew how she often missed things right under her nose...just keep looking...be systematic. Her eyes began an inch by inch methodical exploration, method, a meager comfort. She spotted a belt on the side of the van front of him. She gently tugged the taut belt. No give...she sat back...try it again a little more firmly. She gave it a harder tug. The Plain Woman turned around toward Thomas, a look of apprehension on her face, fine hair on her upper lip visible in the light shining from the van window. She mumbled something apologetically.

They stared at each other, reflections of mortification.

Thomas looked away in an attempt to reconnoiter the situation. That's when she noticed that the belt that she was pulling was already strapped around The Plain Woman. This was the belt for the seat in front of her. What could Thomas have been thinking? A jolt of shame shot through her body. "I'm so sorry. It's my silly mistake."

The Plain Woman looked back gratefully, the transgression no longer hers. She turned around to face forward as if nothing had happened. Thomas stared out the window as the van departed the airport. Almost by chance she noticed the buckle behind her. Of course that makes sense. What was she thinking? Of course it would be buckled from behind…it's okay…it really is okay.

A few of miles of nondescript buildings and scattered palms too straggly to be sentinels, then dark bony mountains thrust up through the sandy desert; tidy shopping malls lay at their feet. The Plain Woman began talking in a confessional tone to her Glamorous Companion. Thomas sat opening the book on his lap with relief. "That she should have walked three miles so early in the day, in such dirty weather, and by herself, was incredible to Mrs. Hurst and Miss Bingley: and Elizabeth was convinced that they held her in contempt for it." Thomas smiled at the thought of Elizabeth's audacity; how brave of her. Thomas looked up from the book…women can do some very daring things, not with overblown male grandeur, but just ordinary important things like visiting a sister when she's sick even if she have to walk. Yes, Thomas is on old woman, an old woman; why, who knows how audacious an old woman can be when she no longer has to be pretty… dressing in purple even…living from the inside…she smiled slightly and began watching the two women in front of him.

The Glamorous Woman perched her sunglasses up in her curly blond hair; the mirrored lens still glittered like a pair of eyes atop her head. She smiled expansively and began regaling her more reticent companion with some sort of story.

The Plain Woman listened in awe.

Thomas closed the book on her lap.

Finally, as if a story, at least an escapade had been told, the Glamorous Woman waited for some kind of response.

The Plain Woman nodded her head emphatically and gratefully. There was a pause. Finally the Plain Woman began talking, her head held motionless. The words were unintelligible to Thomas, but the monotone voice dragged on in some kind of timid lament.

The Glamorous Woman periodically nodded with exaggerated sympathy, as if this tale of sadness somehow confirmed her glamorous status.

The Plain Woman stared at her companion with unquestioning trust.

Thomas, the silent audience to their dialogue, frowned; she wanted The Plain Woman to do something, to do anything other than sit there and be so submissive. Thomas wanted to tap her on the shoulder and tell her that the blond woman was really just afraid and hiding under her synthetic glamour.

The Plain Woman continued her confession as cactuses floated across the windows. Thomas looked away. Why does she care so much? They're just doing what the know how to do, even The Glamorous Woman. What's Thomas doing writing the biography of two complete strangers as if she were the author of their stories. The story of her own life was confusing enough. Her hands tightly clasped the book on her lap. She shook her head and began studying the back of The

Plain Woman's head; the sluggish princess with hair on her upper lip still waiting to be rescued; afraid to be a woman on her own; yes so very familiar. This may not be her story, but was it Thomas'?

The stores along the highway seemed to be multiplying; they must be on the outskirts of Tucson. Her two companions had grown silent. Occasionally The Plain Woman would glance at The Glamorous Woman for reassurance. Thomas sat alone, a ghost. Does Joe really want her to be in Tucson anyway? She could be home reading a biography, if she really wanted to be daring. Her hand scrambled into her pocket and then pulled out her crumpled sheet of paper. She studied the paper intensely…she's supposed to get off at the last stop…she can't make a mistake with that. The Plain Woman started confessing again; The Glamorous Woman smiled knowingly. Tacky buildings, some with Christmas lights…must be getting close. The bus stopped by a shopping mall that appeared to be at the edge of the city. The two women stood up, crouching down so they wouldn't hit their heads. The Glamorous Woman now looked preoccupied by something outside the window. The Plain Woman plaintively called out, "Can we keep in touch?"

The Glamorous turned around, smiling benignly, "There's no reason why we can't do that."

The Plain Woman looked grateful and scribbled a phone number on a piece of paper. She thrust it urgently at her glamorous companion.

The Glamorous Woman looked at it blankly and

then folded it, casually dropping it into her purse. She led the way out.

As the two women waited to get their luggage, The Glamorous Woman casually handed a business card to The Plain Woman. Thomas could see The Plain Woman render a meek and grateful thank you.

A car honked, the Glamorous Woman looked down self-consciously, straightening her dress, and then flashed a dazzling smile at the rough looking man waiting impatiently for her in the truck.

The Plain Woman watched with admiration.

Just before getting into the truck, The Glamorous Woman glanced up at the van perhaps even noticing Thomas. Then the van started moving once again, moving through the city, low buildings crowding the streets; the sun edged toward the horizon leaving shadows behind. She took a deep breath, eyes wide as she hummed a strange melody. The van pulled into a parking lot half filled with other vans. This must be it, the end of the line. The van stopped in front of a building that looked like a cross between a corral and a grocery store. She peered out the window hoping to see Joe or somebody waiting for her…hungry all of a sudden.

The driver announced, "Last stop!"

Thomas sighed with relief. She couldn't miss it; Joe was right. Knapsack on her back she followed the passengers and stepped down onto the soil of Tucson… evening, soft cool air, alone, her voice kept humming that funny little melody all on its own. She watched the remaining passengers take their luggage from the van driver and then hand the driver a tip. Thomas paused stuck on the horns of a moral dilemma...should she slip into the baggage line and give a tip? She had spent $27.50 already today and she didn't have baggage. She stood frozen there in the sweet Tucson evening, her face a battle ground...another moral dilemma, a test to fail...no wonder no one waited for her. She turned her back on the baggage line and took a few slow steps toward the corral/store...forget about the dilemma... keep moving, another test, failed. She may not have believed in the sequence of time, but she most certainly did believe in the sequence of her moral failures.

She looked up from the morass of her sins. A middle-aged handsome man with gray hair and a kind face was sitting on a chair on the porch of the corral. Maybe this is Richard...Thomas flashed on the Glamorous Woman rushing to the arms of her rescuer...such a perfect solution to confusion. Thomas anxiously blinked at the handsome stranger...how would Richard know what Thomas looked like? What if they missed each other; Thomas might miss her chance to be rescued. Her steps slowed. She looked down at her wrist; it ached from squeezing *Pride and Prejudice* so hard. She stopped, staring off into the evening. Elizabeth Bennet never waited, at least not until the end of the book. She just lived her life as well as she could. How strange it would be to live so simply, not like The Glamorous Woman and not like The Plain Woman...just belonging here and now. she paused briefly in front of the Handsome

Stranger…no response…a strange relief. Thomas' face reanimated as her senses opened to the evening… the whir of the traffic…car headlights twinkling on, searching through the twilight…Thomas standing alone in city 2,000 miles from home…that tune she was humming again…what is that tune? Her lips moving trying to find the words…yes, that's it…"I pity the poor immigrant who wishes he would have stayed home"… Bob Dylan. Maybe she was that pitied immigrant, but something in the cool night air awakened her to another proposition.

She focused on the direction her feet were leading, her feet. Maybe she could pick up a sandwich inside the corral-store…hunger…such a simple sensation. She opened the corral door. Instead of a lunch counter or even a country store, two middle-aged women behind a ticket counter glanced at him, a bus ticket counter, no food, just Thomas in the evening far from home. She quickly closed the door, walked across the porch hardly noticing The Handsome Man. She stepped off the porch into the spooky evening. He's, she's an old woman, remember? They don't wait to be saved; they dress in purple. The hummingbirds flickered as Thomas metamorphosed.

Hungry…yes…Richard or Joe could wait. Across the street she noticed a shop with a big bowl of noodles painted on a sign above it. Yes, backpack on her shoulders, Thomas set out with the determination of an arctic explorer. As she approached the restaurant, the mirage of a friendly, mom-and-pop Japanese noodle shop faded; it was a fast food chain restaurant all vinyl and glass with young college students behind the counter. This will do, lovely to be making a decision and do something besides waiting to be rescued. She grabbed a hold of a plastic bamboo handle attached to a dirty glass door and pushed; she stepped through the door into the sound of rap music blaring...a smell half sweet and half rancid. One young man was studying behind the counter and the other stood in a back room leaning against a wall looking bored.

Thomas studied the plastic coated fading pictures of the various dishes above the counter. Her hand reflexively touched her wallet. She'd pick the cheapest one with vegetables; not that she liked vegetables, but she knew she should eat some after having pretzels for lunch. The young man looked up from his book, resigned to his task. Thomas placed her order. The other young man glanced at Thomas sullenly. She heard the sound of a microwave turn on in the back room as she sat down in a booth by the window watching evening settle into Tucson. A lonely string of Christmas lights draped over a cactus in front of the restaurant flashed on and blinking in time to the pounding music. One of the young men placed a plastic tray in front of her, containing mushy looking noodles with a few scraps of meat and grayish broccoli smothered in a brown mucousy sauce. Thomas thanked the young man who was already retreating behind the counter. There, Thomas sat, the only customer in the restaurant... wearing purple. She smiled.

She twirled the last droopy noodle on her fork and swallowed it with, if not with relish, at least satisfaction… she had to pee. She got up and headed toward a shadowy hallway. Rest rooms are usually in shadowy hallways, and there it was.

Sitting on the toilet she released a stream of urine, proud of her resourcefulness. She was doing what she wanted in a strange city thousands of miles from home and no Man in sight. This wasn't so bad.

She strolled more confidently back to the corral and a pay phone on the wall. The handsome stranger was gone like a dream. Plenty of change in her pocket… lucky day…okay, just keep moving. She took a deep breath, pulled out the crumbled piece of paper. She dialed Joe's number; an answering machine took up the call. Joe wasn't home yet. As her hard won bravado evaporated she dialed the mysterious Richard's number. She heard someone pick up the receiver. There was a long silent pause. She heard her own voice mutter tentatively, "Hello?"

A young confident masculine voice answered at the other end. "Hello." There was just a hint of impatience.

Another pause, another puzzle for Thomas. "My name is Thomas and Joe said that I could call Richard when I got into town, because Joe might not be in town yet, and maybe Richard might…" Her voice trailed off into a wisp and then disappeared. Thomas was in free fall.

Just as Thomas' voice vanished, the other voice answered in a business like way. "Yes, Richard just left to pick Joe up at the airport. I'll call his cell and let him know you're here."

Thomas wanted to apologize, but he remembered the apologetic Plain Woman, and just said, "Thank you very much. It is so nice of you to do that."

"Sure," the voice answered abruptly. "I'm Vance."

Thomas was just about to say, "Nice to meet you," as the line went dead.

Thomas sat down in the chair under the light, the same chair that the handsome man had been sitting in; she opened her book and began reading. Another van stopped in front of the corral and deposited people in the parking lot. If anyone had looked up they would have noticed a handsome man casually reading a book under a light on the porch.

"'I hope my dear,' Said Mr. Bennet to his wife, as they were at breakfast the next morning, 'That you have ordered a good dinner today, because I have reason to expect an addition to our family.'" Staring at the page, pieces began coming together. Vance sounds young and confident, probably Richard is too...two handsome men knowing Joe...what's Thomas doing in this picture? She studied the open page of her book...just scribblings across the page...no part for her in there, let alone in Tucson...crazy she-man dreaming all the time. She looked up, her lips mouthing silent words, "I will wear purple, I will wear purple, I will wear purple." She felt a soft breeze touching her cheeks...so different than Minneapolis...wonderful to be sitting outside without freezing her ass off. She nodded to herself...a strange dream. Hers hands closed the book on hers lap. She stared off into the darkness.

"Tom." A voice called through the haze of her imagination.

Thomas looked up studying the shape in the darkness…a shadow about twenty feet away was waving at her. Her eyes focused…a short male form…a familiar dream beckoning, but whose dream?

"Tom," This time the voice called out with more urgency.

She remembered the dream now…Joe, that funny smile of his that said everything is going to be all right even when it wasn't, "Joe."

Chapter 6

Thomas focused on the image, Joe materializing, an Annunciation even after all these years. She rose from the chair leaving it rocking...a hypnotic rhythm in the night. Time and space melted into... was it a dream, or a ghost that was and will always be there hovering around Thomas...a constant...she was drawn toward the smiling apparition. Her body jerked slightly as if something that had been dormant inside her were awakening. She stopped midway down the stairs, pausing for an instant. Then she turned around, ran up the stairs and picked up her knapsack. She spun around to see if the image was still there...yes, Joe. Now that her dream was secured, she suddenly dropped her head in embarrassment. She stood motionless wandering if she was really embarrassed or just acting out a script.

Joe took another step closer.

Thomas glanced at Joe with sly apology, "Don't want to forget this." Thomas held up her knapsack.

Joe made a face of mock irritation. "Pig Face...." Irony and tenderness entwined in Joe's voice. Joe's short form beckoned Thomas into the night.

Thomas followed.

Thomas began noticing details: the thin form with a graying worn face, those eyes still tender and sad and devious.

The gravity of memory drew them together in the parking lot. They both squinted at each other sorting out past and present and future.

Thomas, an embarrassed clown, plodded clumsily forward. "Joe."

Joe's squinting face relaxed. "You made it."

They stopped a foot apart.

"Ya, I did."

"Pigface." Joe shook his head, but tenderly grabbed Thomas' backpack.

"Hummingbirds."

"Come on, Richard's here."

"Ya, I suppose so."

Thomas' body tightened into a formal pose. "Thank you very much." Even her voice sounded formal. She followed; she was in her usual position a few steps behind Joe.

They silently approached what looked like an old jeep. Thomas could see a bearded, strong looking face watching them from the driver's side. What in the hell was Thomas doing here? She studied that face more closely. It was smiling. Thomas took a deep breath.

Joe nodded toward the face. "This is Richard." Joe opened the back door and hopped in with the backpack.

Richard pushed the front door open. "Come on in."

Thomas looked apologetic. "I can sit in back." She paused as if waiting for permission.

Richard waved Thomas in with benign impatience. "How was your trip?"

Words spun around dizzily in Thomas' head; all she could manage was a crazy smile. Glancing sideways she studied Richard; a youngish, strong looking, handsome man in a tank top, his body just beginning to expand into a beefy, not unattractive middle age.

Richard smiled over his tattooed shoulder at Thomas. "Good to meet you." The voice had an easygoing friendly tone.

Thomas looked down innocently; the music of Richard's voice was reassuring even if he was showing too much skin for a cool night. Thomas stepped into the jeep slamming the door behind her. The jeep shuddered with the force of the blow; something clanged inside the door. Thomas cringed and eyed Joe sheepishly.

Joe frowned.

Trying to look as meek as possible Thomas looked over at Richard. "I think I might have broken something."

Richard glanced at Joe...some brief message.

Joe looked back apologetically.

Thomas took it all in, her face prickly with heated embarrassment.

Richard looked calmly at Thomas, "It's an old car. Things break all the time; it's held together by paper clips."

Thomas, inconsolable, grabbed at the door handle; it flopped uselessly in her hand like a broken bird wing. Panic rising, she pushed the door softly with his shoulder. Her whole body was prickly hot now... romance, hummingbirds, time, nothing mattered except being trapped in her own foolishness. On the pearl necklace of time she was stuck on this horrible bead forever.

Richard watched her. "It's all right. I'll open the door from the outside when you two get out."

"Gee I'm sorry...sometimes I just...." Thomas' voice disappeared into abject silence.

Joe, with a familiar smile, benevolence and irony mixing, glanced first at Richard and then settled on Thomas. "I can't take you anywhere."

Thomas smiled back sheepishly. "Here I am in Tucson for ten minutes and I've already broken your door."

"It's nothing, welcome to Tucson." Richard smiled benignly; how could anyone this ridiculous be competition.

Thomas glanced back at Joe with just a hint of theatrical exaggeration. "I promised myself I wouldn't embarrass you this trip."

"You promised." Joe teased.

They both smiled sneakily at each other...some hidden pact.

Thomas settled back in his seat, quietly then turned around to Joe again. "Do you remember the taxi in New York?"

"Oh God!" Joe shook his head and turned away in mock horror. "The taxi!"

With the slightest hint of a teasing smile on her face, Thomas watched Joe.

They stared at each other in a silent standoff, quietly laughing.

For a second Thomas was surprised to see Richard there.

Richard, bewildered by the laughter, glanced for reassurance at Joe.

Thomas quickly took charge and became a self-deprecating clown. She made meek eye contact with Richard. "I was visiting Joe in New York...the first time after I left the city. He met me at the airport, and we were riding in a taxicab to the old apartment that we used to live in together. The taxi stopped in front of the apartment building; everything seemed exactly as I remembered it...everything as usual, and here I was sitting on the driver's side in the back seat. I opened the door...CRASH! A car just happened to be speeding by...I hadn't noticed it." She looked straight into Richard's eyes with shock embarrassment and just the slightest hint of tongue in cheek melodrama.

Richard still looked bewildered.

This was Thomas' cue. "There goes the taxi door, dragged down the street...Yikes!"

Joe spasmed with laughter.

Thomas' giggling transformed into hysteria.

Richard was becoming alarmed.

Thomas caught that look of confusion, that look of being outside the loop. She sobered up. "Don't mind us...just memories from another lifetime.

Richard smiled limply.

Thomas did her best impersonation of a gracious old aunt. "It's so nice of you to pick me up. Joe has told me so many wonderful things about you."

Richard looked pleased.

Thomas smiled benignly...I will wear purple, I will wear purple.

Joe took the cue and talked to Richard as if they were alone in the car...something about antiques that they were selling together.

As the car wound its way through the dark city streets, Joe and Richard chatted on amiably, and Thomas sat, quite content to stare out at the passing lights. The storefronts gave way to shadowy suburban ramblers, haunted *Leave It to Beaver* houses, gravel instead of grass in the front yards. Here and there a lone prickly cactus stuck out of a yard, like sullen disturbing memories of the desert. Streets curled around the barren flat neighborhoods with thirsty whimsy. In the dark scape a few windows flickered with the ghostly glow of television sets, paint peeling from windowsills, prefabricated structures that once passed for modern.

Periodically strings of Christmas lights were draped halfheartedly over boulders or cacti, nostalgia for Christmas somewhere else.

The car slowed in front of one of those dark houses and pulled up into the driveway. Thomas studied the house trying to distinguish it from the houses around it; she scratched her head. The car glided to a stop under a car park. Joe and Thomas still in their conversation stepped out of the car. Thomas made one feeble motion to open the broken door and then sat back to watch patiently behind the barrier of her door.

Joe and Richard's dark shapes stood inches apart. Thomas watched the gap between the shadowy forms closing. This is Joe's new life after all.

The two forms outside suddenly looked up as if they had just remembered something slightly disturbing.

"Let me get the door." Good-naturedly Richard rushed over and released the hostage.

Thomas had a benign befuddled expression on her face. "What an interesting neighborhood." She gingerly stepped out of the jeep. "These are the kind of houses that I grew up with. Of course people had grass and turned the lights on inside more."

Joe and Richard then once again gravitated to each other the way lovers do.

Thomas moved toward the entryway to the house as inconspicuously as possible.

Silhouettes of Joe and Richard melted together in the night…hello young lovers wherever you are.

Not wanting to embarrass them, Thomas turned

sideways and studied the faded wooden trim around the front door. It's so nice that she and Joe have stopped torturing each other.

Richard held Joe in a silent embrace.

Thomas could just barely make them out from the corner of her eye. Richard must certainly be in love. Thomas released a sigh of relief. People in love are forgiving of things like broken doors…in love; it had been a long time, not that she necessarily missed it, but still the wistful longing…

The two shadows began separating. Richard casually informed Joe that he and Vance would be by in a couple of hours and then stepped into the jeep…some sort of plan already made before the arrival of Thomas.

Joe nodded in approval.

The car now backed down the driveway.

Thomas taking one last inspecting look at the woodwork turned toward the retreating car and waved like some daft aunt.

The shadow of Richard's arm waved back.

Joe, backpack slung over his shoulder, walked towards Thomas. For an instant they made quick eye contact, some sort of acknowledgment passed back and forth with the slightest of nods, the merest flicker. The jeep sputtered down the road.

"Here we are." Joe led the way to the door in silence. He reached into his pocket, pulled out keys. They jangled into the lock.

The two shadowy forms disappeared into the dark

house. "Richard seems really nice. You seem to like him, too."

Shadows made confidentiality easier for Joe. Even so there was a wary pause. "He's a nice man."

"He looks like he's in love with you."

"I'm seeing his partner too."

"Oh…" Thomas reminded herself about being the old aunt. She smiled benignly.

"Sometimes, they need me for their relationship too…it gets a little complicated sometimes."

"Most of the time it's okay?"

"Yeh."

They both stood motionless for a heartbeat; then Joe switched the light on and softly handed the backpack to Thomas.

Light exploded into Thomas's eyes. She closed her eyes for a moment; she's here now; she reached for her backpack…she's here…cement floor painted mustard yellow…interesting color….worn turquoise colored sofa, actually a smaller and a larger sofa making an "L" shape…a black and pink pole lamp, like a black and pink skinny sculpture standing at attention at one end of the "L"…a broad mirrored coffee table with a tall avocado green vase and a plastic bag of dried herbs… an old fashioned TV on a TV stand…on one wall, shelves thick with books and found objects including a puppet Thomas once made for Joe…the other wall lined with paintings: images floating on the rough plywood, scratched and painted over as if caught in some kind of process of nervous metamorphosis. She looked approvingly at Joe. "I like your place."

Smiling, looking down, Joe said, "Bum house."

"You seem happy."

Joe stood motionless nodding slightly. "Let me give you the tour."

"Swell."

They stepped into the kitchen of a 1960's housewife gone mad, windowsill over the sink lined with fuzzy haired trolls, Buddha's, rocks, a smiley face button, and an empty bottle of beer. Through the window tall brown grasses, cacti and grapefruit trees crowded together. The sink was embedded in the glory of a maroon and black vinyl counter top on which were placed a whole array of vinegar and oil bottle. A large pink bowl with stale popcorn in it testified to some evening of pleasure before the trip. Old-fashioned picture plates hung on the gray walls. The mustard colored floor anchored the room.

Thomas brushed her admiring hand over the maroon vinyl. "What's the other guy like?"

"Vance…you'll meet him this evening. We don't have as much in common. But it wouldn't work with Richard if he weren't with Vance."

Thomas glanced at Joe, a kind of open-ended glance…careful that it wasn't judgmental…studied, learned neutrality.

Joe caught it and continued. "Richard's worried that Vance hasn't been interested in having sex with him lately…it just wouldn't work without him."

With a very thoughtful look Thomas studied the maroon vinyl again. "It sounds a little complicated."

"It wasn't...for a while." Joe laughed raising his eyebrows

Thomas nodded. "Richard seems to care about you."

"Here's the studio." He motioned toward another door. Thomas followed. They walked into a make shift enclosed porch looking out over the tall grasses, cacti and a grapefruit tree. The floor was plain cement and paintings leaned against the walls as if they had just been completed. Joe pointed to one painting hanging on the wall...a can of brushes on the floor below it waiting to be taken up. "I'm working on this one." He glanced self-consciously at Thomas.

Thomas was lost among all the paintings, Red Riding hood in awe at the forest of pictures around her. She was wandering from one to the other...strange oval shapes floating in fields of color, layer upon layer of color that had been scratched, piling up through time. The shapes seemed to be traveling and growing, not moving through space, but through time. She glanced up at the unfinished painting. "I like them. That's not finished yet?"

They were in the woods together now. Joe searched the unfinished painting intensely. "No...I worked on it the night before I left." He looked down apologetically. "I show them at a gallery...Helena, she owns the gallery, really pushes me. I need that." He walked over to a desk covered in papers and cups and little statues. He pressed the button of an answering machine. A very definite and exacting voice filled the speaker. "Hey Joe. This is Helena. Will you call me as soon as you get back? I want to know how you're doing with the paintings for the exhibit. Call me."

Joe looked over at Thomas. "You see."

Thomas grinned. "More power to her."

They looked at each other with the familiarity of a secret joke.

Joe mimicked remorse. I'm a bum."

"Better a manager than a partner."

Joe looked away and out the window. "My garden."

"Looks wonderful…kind of wild."

Joe nodded with satisfaction. "Check it out if you want."

"Ya." Thomas stared out the window, her feet shuffling with excitement. "You know me and gardens."

"You like them more than people."

"I do?" Thomas looked bewildered.

"They're so stationary."

"This is a neat place. It somehow fits you."

"Whore Joe," he looked down in exaggerated shame.

Thomas tried to look him in the eyes. "I don't regret anything about the time we spent together except maybe how I kept judging you."

Joe shook his head. "I wasn't very nice."

"And I was holding on to you for dear life because I didn't know how to live my own life. It drives me crazy now when people do that to me."

They looked each other for a flickering instant.

Joe walked back into the kitchen. "I'll show you

your bedroom." He looked limp. "It's nap time for me. I'll be up in a couple of hours."

Back through the crazy kitchen and the 1960's living room and into a shadowy hallway, Joe switched on the light illuminating a mattress on the mustard floor, neatly made up with blankets and sheets; towels and a washcloth lay in a neat pile on the corner of the bed. Joe motioned toward the bed. "Make yourself at home. You even have your own bathroom." He pointed to a shadowy little room off the bedroom.

Thomas said, "Swell," absentmindedly. She was staring at a whole gallery of faces staring back at her. Two of the bedroom walls were covered with pictures of huge-eyed children and puppies all looking out on the world with pouty sadness. Some even had precious teardrops glistening on their velvet cheeks. They stared out inconsolable and at the same time understanding how cute they really looked. She plopped the knapsack down on the mattress.

Joe ignored the gallery. "Richard was fucking a guy here he met this weekend.

Thomas looked squeamish.

"He changed the sheets."

Thomas forced a smile. Pictures flooded into her mind...what if one of them had crabs...she remembered trying to get rid of them for three weeks in New York... she felt them crawling over her body...relax... it'll be okay...what if she brought crabs home? Relax...you ruined his door. Thomas nodded at Joe.

"Bedtime for Bonzo." Joe smiled drowsily at Thomas

and headed toward his bedroom. "Make yourself at home. See you a little later."

Thomas stood motionless in the middle of the room…maybe she shouldn't crawl under the covers… or even sit on the bed…you're gonna be here all week… that doesn't make sense…don't think about crabs. She walked toward the shadowy bathroom. When in doubt, pee. She switched the bathroom light on. Pictures of paint-by-number animals covered the walls. A shelf around the ceiling held the kind of ceramics people used to put on their new television sets when Thomas was a boy…when she was a he. Surrounded by all those animals Thomas pulled her pants down, sat on the cool toilet seat, and stared back at the animals. Her whole body began releasing as the toilet bowl echoed the tinkling sound. She smiled tentatively in the midst of the animal kingdom.

First she sat on the edge of the bed…this isn't so bad. Tiredness swept over her and the pillow looked so inviting. What the hell! She kicked off her shoes leaving her socks on, pulled down hers pants like a snakeskin… tired. She slipped under the cool sheets; her head rested on the pillowy cloud. That's that, crabs or no crabs. She'll sort out any problems later. Her imagination was evaporating, her head sinking deeper and deeper… grayness…

Chapter 7

Thomas woke up, the overhead light still on; pieces of the present fell into place under the sad eyes of children who knew they would never get what they needed but could use their deprivation to create poignant charm...window dark with night...the last call of a desert bird...Tucson...Joe...Danny...crabs... five days in a strange place...Joe. Thomas sat up, wide awake, and listened for sounds in the strange house... all quiet...Joe sleeping...bedtime for Bonzo. One of the things that Thomas used to hate was the way Joe would disappear into sleep or drinking or affairs and leave Thomas bereft and all alone...this empty hole, dizzy and dark and bottomless...all she could do was wait, terror and anger swirling, waiting for the reassuring sound of Joe's keys jingling in the lock or the sound of the toilet flushing. She rubbed her cheek; the whisper of a day old beard reassured her back into the present.

God, that was a time ago…hundreds of miles worth of time…all flickering away.

She slipped on her pants and shoes with the secret excitement of a child getting up early on Christmas morning…a whole evening, a whole week to explore a place where hardly anybody knew her. Her body sat still; all the possibilities of this week coiled within her like other dimensions…such an extraordinary inter-dimensional creature, potential, an amphibian straddling today and tomorrow. She winked at the pouting children staring out at her from their walls.

She quietly walked to the door leading to the hallway, peeking into the slightly open door of Joe's bedroom…soft regular breathing sounds…how lovely…. warm floors under stocking feet. Thomas stepped silently into the hallway; her steps barely whispering in the gloom. Straight ahead was a shadowy room that she hadn't noticed, a mysterious chamber. She walked in; it took a moment for her eyes to focus in on objects. It was a dining room, small with a large window looking out over the haunted garden. The moon shone cool blue drenching everything in the room. Objects were so saturated by the moonlight that they appeared to be imbued with an inner life. The furniture, things Joe must have found on his scavenger hunts, glowed with the afterlife of its previous owners, whispering softer than Joe's breathing, alive. The soft pads of Thomas' fingers brushed against the smooth cool surface of a mirror-topped dining room table, the black mirror opened up into a bottomless well, a worm hole to who knows where. Her whole hand pressed against the surface, listening for stories…her life with Joe had been filled with dark mirrors…no way to grab anything, but only fall through like Alice…tumbling down…when the worst happens, you end out somewhere else. Her face grimaced slightly. People recognized that Joe lived in a magic universe, everything around him imbued with mystery. But as soon as you grabbed at Joe to hold the magic, he disappeared or even worse did some innocent act of retribution for the loss of his freedom. Thomas lifted her hand suddenly, as if withdrawing it from something hot.

She took a deep breath, and continued her exploration…four padded thrones around the dark shiny well, each throne held a shadow guarding the mystery of the mirror. She pushed the throne next to her; it spun around, ghost and all, with a faint sibilant "sssh." Standing at one corner of the table was a four-foot tall plaster statue…a renaissance servant boy waiting patiently to serve his betters. Looming on a wall above the table, a large picture of "The Blue Boy" held court, so perfectly, completely, ungraspably, two dimensional. Was that innocent opaque look boredom, condescension, or simply the resigned look of someone trapped, frozen in his universe?

The faint murmur of the refrigerator led her into the dark kitchen, past the bowl of ancient popcorn, and into the studio. In the moonlight the shapes in the paintings floated in and out of time. Though imprisoned on flat wood, frozen in space, they exercised their freedom in time and memory…like fish in an aquarium, their images playing on the brittle two-dimensional surface, playing on the flat screen, another dimension trying to break through.

The moon drew her out of the pictures and led her feet across the cement floor, through a softly complaining screen door and out into the garden. A world opened…tall grasses trembling with the rhythm of a night wind, big globular grapefruit hanging so heavily that Thomas could hear the trees straining to hold on to their burdens. A train faintly rumbled in the distance. She looked up, stars and moon falling into the impossible darkness, and steadied herself, hers hand grasping something rubbing against her leg: canvas, stretched over the wire frame of a chair to form wings like a moth, a pouch stretched beneath the wings, something to sit on, riding a moth through the night sky. Three other moths, one with a tattered wing, all had landed around a rusting a metal table with skinny legs. On it an aluminum bud of a vase was beginning to open like a night flower.

A siren blasted from somewhere beyond the garden… the present, so vulnerable or persistent. In alarm the globed grapefruit tugged harder at the branches. In sympathy Thomas walked towards the tree to give whatever feeble support she could, placing her hand softly under a grapefruit, calming it. She could feel the warmth of the sun still contained.

Hers duty done, she followed the curve of the path

through piles of stones, ceramic pots, bleached bones. Were they markers or warnings?

She stepped back into the studio; the phone rang jangling away the ghosts. Should she answer it...you always answer phones...or do you? She walked briskly over to the ringing sound. The phone sat on a desk in the studio...the fourth ring...an answering machine switched on. "Hello Joe, this is Tim, welcome back."

Thomas took a step back afraid to be an eavesdropper, but she listened all the same.

"I'm having a cocktail party here tomorrow evening. Would you like to come? You could bring Thomas. Let me know." The faintest hint of urgency underlay that voice.

Another ghost entered the quiet house, the fluttering of wings. Tim...Joe's partner after Thomas, the person Joe moved to Tucson with...that faint hint of love and anger in the voice on the answering machine...another ex. Love ends so slowly, diminishing like a radioactive half-life, into eternity. Tim seemed so smart, attractive, so absolutely together when Joe introduced him to Thomas.

As if summoned out of a dream, Joe's shadowy shape walked drowsily into the dark room. His shadow said, "Do you want a beer?"

Thomas tried to sound as benign as she could. "Thanks...sure."

The two ghosts made eye contact, sparks in the darkness.

Joe shuffled over to the refrigerator. He sighed deeply

as if opening the refrigerator door were a daunting task. His hand pulled at the door; it opened. The light from the belly of the refrigerator flooded Joe's body, light burnishing his face and hands, a Rembrandt painting: "Man Opening the Refrigerator". The door closed; once again he stood in darkness. One shadow handed presented a bottle of beer to Thomas.

The coolness of the bottle in her hand woke Thomas up…Tucson…vacation…two middle aged people in a kitchen…Danny somewhere on another planet. She took a swallow of beer, the taste of cool tears running down her throat numbing her. She remembered that Joe didn't like to talk when he was tired, and he barely liked to talk when he wasn't. Thomas took another long swallow. She certainly didn't want to bring up anything about the message; rest in peace. She nodded to no one in particular and walked out of the room. She switched a lamp light on in the living room, setting up hers own private little orbit. As if waiting for her, there sat her book; she must have put it there when she came in. Her hands opened the pages at the bookmark. "Elizabeth, having rather expected to affront him, was amazed at his gallantry, but there was a mixture of sweetness and archness in her manner which made it difficult for her to affront anybody: and Darcy had never been so bewitched by any woman as he was by her. He really believed, that were it not for the inferiority of her connections that he would be in some danger."

Joe, his footsteps now more animated, walked into the living room. "Tim just left a message. Do you want to go to a cocktail party tomorrow?" Joe sounded like someone conveying information about troubling weather.

"A cocktail party?" Thomas looked as uncomplaining as she was able and smiled tentatively. Not only must she deal with Richard and Vance...and now Tim, but a cocktail party filled with more handsome younger men with opinions about everything, competent, confidently milling about a room, saying the right things to each other, laughing at the right times. She tried not to sound anxious. "I don't know...I...I guess I'm game."

Joe looked thoughtful and then frowned...he always wanted some else to say no or goodbye.

Thomas froze in place, a far off look on her face that she hoped would cover up what was going on inside...she wasn't going to be left holding the bag for the decision this time.

Joe turned away and stood silently.

Into that still room a large black long-haired cat cautiously crept, each step as silent as a secret.

Joe smiled; once again animated; he crouched down. "Puss, Puss."

The cat paused on its quiet journey. With elegant calm it turned its head toward Joe and made an intimate little singsong sound.

Joe smiled.

The cat turned its head back.

Thomas closed the book.

The cat caught the moving form. Her whole body transformed, hair sticking out on end, back arching.

Jolts of electricity coursed through her body. She blasted out a screeching yowl and rocketed across the living room, into the kitchen, into the studio, and finally into the garden. All that was left of her was the sound of a cat door banging shut.

Thomas scrunched down in remorse.

For the briefest instant, faster than the speed of light, Joe shot a crazy angry glance at Thomas.

Thomas, who could see the flicker of painted humming birds, caught the flash, her body trembling in an orgy of remorse. "I'm so sorry."

Joe held the silence, giving the remorse time to blossom. Then he cooed softly, "Puss, Puss, it's okay, it's just Thomas. He won't hurt you." He glanced back at Thomas. "She doesn't like strangers. She's scared of everybody." His voice was now soaked in reassurance.

Thomas played out her remorse just enough to get a dollop more of reassurance. "Here I am taking over her house."

Joe cooed, "Pigface."

Thomas smiled tentatively.

Joe smiled with gracious benevolence. "I'm going to my gallery tomorrow. Do you want to come?"

Thomas reanimated with excitement. "That sounds fun."

"It's a chi-chi gallery." His voice was suddenly self-deprecating, contempt turning back upon himself.

This was Thomas' cue to reassure Joe. "Everything's stupid anyway."

Joe nodded, pleased at the transaction. "You'll see...

sometime after 1PM. I sleep late. Can you take care of yourself til then?""

"Don't be an idiot,"

A few minutes later Joe reappeared. "I called Tim and said maybe—yes for tomorrow night. So tomorrow night it is." He looked relieved. "Do you want to smoke? Richard and Vance will be here in a few minutes. Where do you want to eat?"

Thomas let the questions filter in...imagining herself crazy, anxious and stoned...wide eyed nuts when they came. "I think I'll wait til they get here, so we all start out equal." She looked down as placidly as she could. "I don't care where we go." She held on to her book...tightly.

Joe sat down on the sofa in front of the coffee table, sifting through a bag of marijuana. "Mexican! I've got the perfect place." He glanced over at Thomas with the excitement of a small boy.

That smile, so excited about an adventure brought Thomas back...the time they slept in a cornfield overnight...she smiled at the memory; adventures are easier to deal with in the past. Thomas smiled like the Cheshire Cat. "I'm not gay anymore."

Joe took a long drag of the joint.

"I'm a woman inside."

"You just need a good fuck."

Thomas studied Joe's face under the veil of smoke. "That's what you always said."

"Pigface."

Thomas split in half, not a painful splitting

anymore…the past…the present…two universes she could straddle without being torn apart. For a moment she looked like she was staring at those painted hummingbirds. "It's been really complicated but kind of fun lately. Now that that the dream-come-true of Prince Charming is fading a little, all sorts of other possibilities come up, and some I can even try."

Joe laughed in mock horror. "Thomas the nun."

Thomas smiled. " At least you have the gender right."

"You're just afraid of handsome men. You always go to extremes."

"I said faded a little, besides all that sex stuff is over rated. Even when I was with you; I kept trying to get something that wasn't there."

Joe looked hurt.

"It's not that so much, but I couldn't get what I wanted because I wasn't who I really was."

"What about Danny?"

"I don't know. He may not know it, but he's pretty crazy too. He kind of lets me be and likes it when I take risks. I wouldn't necessarily say I'm happy."

"Happy? When did that mattered to you?"

"You liked me better sad."

"I'm a terrible person.' Joe looked down in sad sack remorse.

Thomas watched him. "This is my cue to take care of you."

"Pigface." Joe looked up slyly.

There was another one of those moments...old friends who drove each other crazy.

Thomas smiled slyly back. "He's got a pretty good sense of humor."

Joe looked skeptical. "I hope so."

"He's got some funny stuff. He started having sex as a kid and it was this real hidden thing. In some ways he's still a kid."

"I leave you alone for a few years and look what a mess you get into."

"Mess..." Thomas's eyes narrowed. "Do you remember us? Maybe Danny and I can actually grow up together."

They stared off at each other at point blank range.

The doorbell rang. They both jumped, startled back into the present. For an instant they looked at each other like scared lost children.

Joe retreated to the door while Thomas stood up at attention, face frozen in panic.

The door opened; two large shapes crowded the doorway.

"It's about time," Joe switched on a flirtatious smile.

Thomas tried to adopt a folksy easy-going attitude, but all she could manage was a wooden spaced out expression.

Richard gave Joe a peck on the cheek. "Look who's talking?" They held each other for an instant.

Vance still stood in the shadows, a dull vague shape. Finally the shape stepped into the house, stiffly moving around Joe and Richard.

Thomas watched the transformation of a shape into a human being…thick shoulders…heavy moving…dark hair with a mustache…a baseball hat turned backwards like a college jock just returned from a ball game…an aloof look on his face…wounded, defensive and alone. Thomas glanced away shyly…the lonely, wounded, handsome image flickering in her imagination…he looks like Darcy when Elizabeth first spotted him… handsome and aloof…it took half a novel for Elizabeth to recognize his true character.

Thomas peeked again at Vance comparing him to Darcy…certainly Darcy wouldn't wear a baseball hat backwards.

Joe glanced at Thomas. "You remember Richard?"

Thomas tried to smile as warmly as she could. "Nice to see you again." That didn't sound threatening. She gave Richard a hug while avoiding looking straight at Vance.

Richard enclosed Thomas in a bear hug.

Thomas felt startled by the pressure and then just for a second relaxed into the embrace.

Vance stood to the side, motionless.

With forced flirtatiousness Joe sidled over to Vance. "Vance this is Thomas."

Thomas glanced over nervously. Vance glanced back even more nervously. Like flopping fish their eyes, slipping and sliding passed each other.

For a moment Thomas didn't know what to do with this vision of maleness, the kind of maleness that seemed as untouchable as the northern star. Finally

Thomas looked away. How would Elizabeth handle this situation? Elizabeth was forthright, feisty, witty, courageous. Thomas' face began to droop as she realized the discrepancy between her heroine and herself.

Vance, true to Darcy's character continued to look uncomfortable.

Thomas with a hint of Elizabeth's courage walked over to Vance and gave him a quick hug.

Vance stood there hardly acknowledging the human contact. His eyes had a faraway look.

Up close Thomas felt the gravitational pull of Vance's masculinity, or was it Darcy's? Thomas looked down at her own hands, certainly not a dainty girl's small hands, middle aged hands with little age spots scattered over the tops. She's not Elizabeth…old hands that have pulled at life desperately…not feisty at all… an old woman wearing purple, yes perhaps. She smiled at Vance with distant kindness of an old aunt.

Both Joe and Richard were watching them closely… some hidden message. Joe finally broke the spell. Hey, do you guys want a smoke?"

Richard made his way to the sofa, "Sounds good."

With some tenderness Joe placed his arm around Vance's waist. "Sit down, make yourself at home."

Vance nodded woodenly.

All four shuffled around the "L" shaped sofa. Joe stationed himself on one end of the "L." Richard quickly sat next to him. Thomas sat down at the other end. Vance sat down, an island equidistant from Richard and Thomas.

Vance's voice blared out as if he were at a great distance. "I went to a bar last night." His voice had a strained quality to it, a public tone, no personal focus, like a radio announcer's voice. "They carded me." He laughed with an edge of high pitched hysteria; then his face quickly froze again.

Thomas listened to Vance. This certainly wasn't Darcy's voice…strained, embarrassed, even false. It was more like the voice of a pretentious Mr. Collins in the body of Mr. Darcy. She wasn't the only incongruous person here. With modest kindness Thomas nodded at Vance.

Vance gulped for air as if he were about to speak again and then swallowed whatever was coming out.

Richard nodded at him with reassurance.

"It made my day." Vance's voice started softer but became strained as he said the last word.

Joe glanced at Vance's hat, "College boy."

Vance let out a high-pitched pleased laugh.

Richard patted Vance in approval and passed a fat joint to him.

Vance glanced at the joint; It was as if there was a gap, a time lapse of a second around Vance. His timing was just a little off. "I wasn't going to…"

Richard lit the joint for him.

Vance took a deep toke, exhaled a white cloud and for an instant appeared relaxed. He tightened up as he glanced at Thomas and obliviously passed the joint to her.

Thomas, who was waiting for some signal of

familiarity, looked down as if she had just failed some kind of test. She hesitantly picked the joint out of Vance's fingers. Thomas took a deep toke... I'm not Elizabeth Bennet...I'm not charming even as an older woman" ...there was only the tightness in her stomach...she exhaled, smoke streaming out of her mouth, veiling herself...yes...smoking joint dangling from her fingers... no beautiful story. Her hand reached across the "L."

Joe was watching her. His hand reached out from his end of the "L" and grasped the joint lightly but surely, a high wire hand off. Joe smiled at Thomas.

Thomas smiled back from behind his veil of smoke...so much safer to have a veil between herself and Joe...safer for both. From her new vantage point Thomas looked at her companions. Their lips curled around their mouths like angle worms, fringes of eye lashes flickering across glassy eyeballs, those two funny looking black holes above the angle worm lips that move ever so slightly with each breath; Jane Austen where are you? She started to giggle softly...the absurdity of mammals.

Richard, taking a deep toke glancing at Thomas with concern and then handed the joint to Vance.

Thomas watched the hands meet...so delicately... under water smooth...maybe people don't really exist... just stories in an aquarium-theater. Her face turned blank with amazement.

A mammal hand with a finger delicately curled around a joint passed into her field of vision. For an instant she was too curious about the event to move…the story of the evening flooded back into her consciousness…she grasped the joint from Vance's digits. Thomas took deep toke, held it… mind spinning…and then released the breath. The bridal veil became thicker.

This time Joe reached out first as if asking for Thomas' hand.

Thomas whispered, "Hello again Jane," and passed off the joint to her suitor. This time behind her veil, instead of seeing the stories she saw the insides of peoples' brains…blood and electrical charges creating reality…too much information. She shook her head and looked at the surfaces of their faces again. They are all younger faces, a veil of years between her and her companions. Joe: six years younger, Richard and Vance: twelve years younger…the universe transforming with age…unintelligible, clumsy, grotesque to younger people especially when eroticism is involved. Her face flushed with embarrassment…her dream of waking up at a party with only her underwear on…nowhere to hide as formally dressed guests enter the room, their heels clicking against the marble floor. Thomas turned her face away from the other three…paranoia…remember… pot of smoking…brain chemistry. Her eyes refocused as she turned back to her companions. She smiled benignly at the three people…this wasn't so bad…like Ulysses listening to the sirens. She was distanced from them now, tied to the mast by her awareness…not terrifying, not really…an adventure. Even though her mouth was dry, she swallowed and said, "That's powerful stuff."

The other three were watched her as the sound of her words echoed over the distance.

Vance handed her the joint again.

Thomas took a shallow toke this time...there are limits to her sense of adventure. She ercomposed himself as she reached across the "L."

Again Joe seemed to anticipate Thomas' hand across the void.

Thomas sat back on the sofa...a Ferris wheel compartment...funny...even though she and Joe never understood each other, they still knew how to reach across.

A voice called from far away, Richard's voice. "Have you stopped by the store?"

From deep inside the sofa Thomas knew that it wasn't only she and Joe that were on the high wire.

Joe shook his head with exaggerated remorse.

"We sold some things." Richard's voice rang with urgency.

"It's all your stuff, nobody wants mine." Joe said in a hangdog teasing way.

Thomas was watching a movie now.

Joe passed the joint back to Richard.

He took a toke.

Richard passed the joint to Vance.

Thomas's face turned impassively to Vance...maybe that's how people stay calm...they're just watching movies...granted that terrible things can happen, but you don't have to look beyond the screen. She watched as Vance took a toke. Maybe it didn't matter that she doesn't have a clue who Vance is or Richard, and even Joe. Maybe understanding isn't so important, or at least not as important as entertainment…nothing more important than an interesting vantage point. She took Vance's pass gracefully. They even made brief eye contact. It's not so bad really not to have any idea of what is going on. She passed the joint along without taking a toke…not lonely or wanting something, but rather a singular vantage point to look out on things with some curiosity…this really is all right.

She glanced with satisfaction at Joe.

Joe, in Richard's orbit glanced back, watching Thomas with a funny smile on his face, perhaps looking out from his vantage point. "I told you about all that 60's stuff I was collecting. It's worth something now…very chic.' He grinned in self-mockery.

Richard joined in, pushing a little closer to Joe. "We both collect it. We have a booth at an antique shop."

Thomas nodded benignly from the distance. "Oh that sounds fun."

Vance announced formally from his distance, "We love the 60's, the forms and colors." He edged closer to Richard.

Richard and Joe glanced at each other. Richard nodded at Vance benignly.

Thomas watched all three of her companions merge into one 60's loving organism. Under the veil of marijuana her mind was weaving in and out in an elaborate dance…Vance seemed so like an orphan… someone who always has to try to fit in and for that very reason can't. Thomas wanted to put her arm around Vance and say that we're okay even if were not popular. It's somehow okay. Then the dance veered wildly and Thomas was swept away wondering what it would be like to touch Vance's thick shoulders…to feel his broad chest. The beat changed again, and now Thomas saw herself as an old preposterous queen…the possibility of being attractive, too funny for words, ridiculous. She halted the dance looking away like a modest girl…a girl, a girl still growing up…maybe a woman someday. What would Vance think about an old girl attracted to him? Masculinity is so fragile.

Vance looked at her blankly repeating. "We love the 60's."

There was an uncomfortable silence; everyone seemed to be looking away from each other. Thomas took charge and looked at Richard. "Thanks for your help this afternoon. I hate to be in your way."

Richard looked over kindly at Thomas. "You weren't in the way. A friend of Joe's came a few weeks ago. That guy was impossible." He glanced over at Vance. They nodded in disdainful communion. "Mike Anderson… he kept following us around and not saying anything; he just couldn't take a hint."

Thomas rose an inch or two from the depths of her mind…Mike Anderson…a different movie began flashing through Thomas' brain…how could she forget Mike Anderson…that innocent oblivious face haunting Joe and Thomas' life together. She whispered, "Mike Anderson."

With a combination of pity and humor Joe echoed, "Mike Anderson."

Vance jumped in. "We went to Phoenix and he invited himself, and then he followed us around... everywhere...he didn't say anything." Vance and Richard exchanged outraged looks.

Thomas nodded her head, her eyes focusing on the movie in her mind...Mike Anderson...years ago he kept moving in with Thomas and Joe...no matter where they went Mike always followed...that quiet innocent bewildered face of Mike's...waiting for something...and everything he touched broke or fell apart...something about Mike always drove Thomas nuts, the periodic intrusions, the way chaos seemed to follow Mike. Then Thomas would feel guilt, guilt, guilt for feeling anger at such an innocent man...to kill a mockingbird.

She surfaced to the Tucson movie...the look on Richard and Vance's faces...condescension, irritation and humor all mixing up in a brew.

The two now turned their gaze on Thomas.

She was no longer sitting in the safe depths of the sofa; her face now stuck out forward as if it were on the prow of a ship...a hot embarrassing tide slowly rose in her body...yes, yes, she was like Mike, so like Mike she couldn't stand it. Perhaps she and Mike lived in the same universe. The hot tide submerged Thomas...she's Mike Anderson...Mike Anderson is herself. Thomas felt the waves smash against herself, against her wooden face.

Vance passed the joint to Thomas.

Thomas picked the joint from Vance's fingers and

passed it across the "L" to Joe. Joe was smiling. Where is he in all of this? Does it really matter? Thomas' body sank back into the sofa...a movie that she doesn't necessarily have to be part of...she can even watch herself in the movie...just watch with curiosity from her vantage point. Maybe that's what Mike was doing. The flood of embarrassment began ebbing. Funny how having a vantage point makes the world seem a little less terrifying. It's not that terrible things can't happen, but at least a portion of awareness doesn't disappear. She's not exactly Mike Anderson after all, but she kind of understands what it might feel like to be Mike. Suddenly there's room for...empathy, yes, that's what empathy is. Thomas smiled, deep inside the sofa. Something magic budded inside her, opening.

Joe was studying Thomas.

Thomas, ironic smile on her face, stared at Richard and Vance and Joe. A disembodied voice, an oracle's voice, issued forth from Thomas. "Be careful, Mike is a magician."

The others, bewildered, stared at her

Thomas remained silent; the three waited in suspense. She peered out from the depths like some mysterious soothsayer. Words issued forth again. "A long time ago, I didn't like Mike either. He frightened me. He was all the things I didn't want to be." Thomas' face hazed over in mystery. She made solemn eye contact with Joe, Richard, and finally Vance. Thomas nodded slowly, "And sure enough twenty years later I'm living in his world, and despite trying so hard to avoid it, I feel what it's like to be him. Be kind to him; it'll help you later, later when it's your turn."

They stared at her, bewildered, a little frightened.

A far away knowing smile flickered across her face, like she was in on some secret. "Mike's magic."

Complete silence, the last butt of the marijuana lay dead in the ashtray. Joe laughed nervously. "Where do you guys want to eat tonight?" Everyone looked vague or maybe just stoned. "How about Mexican?" This wasn't exactly a question since all three took his direction. Joe got up and headed towards the door.

The other three fell into line, first Richard, then Vance, and finally Thomas ambled along in the rear; Joe liked to be in charge. They disappeared out the door, Mike Anderson's ghost watching them.

Joe led the shuffling group through the door and into the restaurant. The wailing of brown skinned middle-aged men in sombreros exploded in their ears; the men were strumming their guitars and walking around the tables packed with Anglo diners. The hostess, a severe eyed woman, her hair long and black except for the spidery grayness at the part in the middle of her head, met them, nodded solemnly, and led them between the crowded tables. She stopped in front of an empty booth. A short dark young man scrambled to clear dirty dishes off the table. The Spider-Haired Hostess stood motionless, oblivious to the young man's frantic maneuvers. He wiped the table off. She surfaced from where ever she had placed her consciousness and nodded to the four guests, bestowing on each a menu. She disappeared never to be seen again.

Thomas looked around for her...funny how things happen, bubbling up out of the present and then disappearing. She stood there, a far off look on her face as her three companions jockeyed for seats...a strange dance in which Joe as usual was the center. The sombreroed singers were rasping a melody that was slowly building in volume. Richard and Joe sat opposite each other. Vance stationed himself next to Richard. Thomas moved into the configuration, next to Joe and opposite Vance. The configuration of four gelled as the momentum of the rasping voices soared into a wailing lament.

Thomas' heart suddenly sailed upwards spinning her around the high ceiling, banqueters clustering beneath her around table islands. The wailing softened into a sad melody. Thomas descended to her position in the booth.

She heard Joe's voice from the distance say grandly, "My treat."

Thomas let go of the sound of the music...Joe's treating again...what would a woman do?

Joe sat back pleased with himself.

Thomas looked across the table at the two men opposite her...yes they were handsome.

Vance glanced matter-of-factly at Joe, "How are the margaritas?"

Joe muttered, "Big."

Richard laughed, "The way you like 'um."

Joe grimaced in exaggerated remorse, "I'm an alcoholic bum."

A moment of silence at the table; Vance and Richard glanced at each other with some subtle understanding. Thomas soared once more as the singers wailed one last time, then a moment of silence in the restaurant. She peeked down from the wooden chandeliers before settling back into the booth...Joe would be treating... he was always treating and confessing.

Thomas gathered her attention, focusing on Joe who sat there in the center, everyone slowly spinning around him, this little haggard looking man with a bristly gray face and dark eyes that always seemed to be hiding something precious.

Joe caught Thomas' stare. "I'm an alcoholic bum."

Again there was that glance between Richard and Vance.

Thomas started giggling... there was a time when Thomas took satisfaction in those confessions. Night after night Joe would come home drunk from some escapade...Thomas frightened and furious. Joe would slowly walk up the stairs to the bed room slumping towards Thomas' form frozen in the bed, "I'm a no good bum." Thomas would melt like snow in April. Joe would slip between the covers, clothes and all, and Thomas, ignoring her fear and anger, would comfort Joe. Then he would look even more remorseful and begin to smile mischievously.

Joe turned to Thomas. "How about you? Do want to go to Margaritaville?"

"I'll take a big one, too."

With mock self-vindication Joe said, "I told you that all you needed was a good fuck."

Vance and Richard watched them cautiously.

"Your answer for everything."

Vance chimed in. "La Casita's are better."

Richard and Vance nodded at each other for reassurance.

Eyeing Thomas, Joe ignored them. "At least I don't spend all my time..." Just then a serious eyed brown skinned woman approached the table timidly. With difficulty she asked for their orders. Richard switched to Spanish. The waitress looked down with embarrassment as if she had failed a test.

Thomas switched into her daft aunt persona. She looked kindly at The Waitress. "I just got here from Minnesota. You wouldn't believe how cold it is there. This is such a lovely climate."

The Waitress smiled shyly.

Joe took over and began ordering.

They drank and ate, words not so very important, especially for Thomas. The other three ordered another margarita; Thomas watched and began drinking lots of water; she hated hangovers. Like a hovering ghost, she didn't have to say anything now and could relish the indistinct blur of people's voices...time out for Thomas. She glanced over at Joe again.

Joe smiled back mysteriously.

The waitress silently filled Thomas' water glass.

Thomas could feel herself slowly surfacing, "Thanks."

Joe put on his glasses; suddenly he looked like an old grandfather; his hands were shaking slightly as he picked up the bill. The guitar music had stopped again while he studied the bill intently.

Thomas studied Joe. Was she taking advantage of Joe? He looked so frail and tipsy. Were the other two? Thomas studied them secretly...two aging boy-men... nothing devious, maybe naive, though they certainly wanted to be sophisticated...and Joe really did like to be grand and devil may care. Besides it was Joe's life, and she, Thomas would take him at his word...keep it simple, always keep it simple with Joe. Thomas would treat Joe to supper some other evening.

There was a moment of silence. Thomas looked down, afraid to be eves dropping on this clumsy moment between the three men...maybe they were just submerged in a drug-induced haze. She studied their vacant faces. She was alone and could do whatever he wanted...whatever struck her fancy. "Why don't you two come over for supper on Monday? I'll cook some spaghetti or something simple." She glanced over at Joe.

Joe nodded, a goofy smile on his face, "Come on over."

Richard and Vance were struggling to surface out of their haze, eyes slowly focusing on Thomas. First Richard, then Vance popped up to the surface.

All three were staring at Thomas...three sets of eyes.

Thomas had a sudden urge to duck back into a rabbit hole, but she knew it was too late.

Joe watched Thomas' budding discomfort; he liked to see Thomas vulnerable.

Thomas turned away slightly, just far enough away so that she wasn't looking at Richard and Vance head on. Time to shift...an old woman...some nuts but benevolent aunt...eccentric even; no one to take too seriously. She faced them again, a kind of spacey Good Witch of the West...what was her name...Glinda? She stared straight at them enveloping them in a glittery smile...yes, burnt preposterous meals were part of her charm.

This time Richard and Vance turned away; Glinda was too much for them.

Thomas had them on the run. Besides she was the only one who was relatively sober. "I'll just throw a little old something together."

Richard and Vance nodded submissively.

Thomas stared them down with a crazy smile. "Never killed anybody yet."

Vance and Richard shuddered.

Joe was catching the whole scene. "Beans!"

Thomas glared back at him archly. "I *like* beans."

Joe was on a role. "Do you remember when Craig from New York came over for one of your masterpieces? He called the next day and said he had been throwing up for twenty four hours."

Thomas looked at Joe with mock alarm. "He had such a delicate stomach."

Vance looked like a cornered rat.

Richard came to the rescue. "That's a really nice offer, but there's lots of things we don't eat."

Thomas melted with accommodating graciousness. "I can manage. What don't you eat?"

Richard looked at Vance. "He doesn't eat fish."

Thomas nodded reassuringly.

Vance looked at Richard. "He doesn't eat red meat."

Thomas sat there nonplussed.

Grasping at straws Richard said, "He doesn't eat mushrooms."

Thomas smiled benignly confident. "That's not so bad."

Vance was sweating. "But he doesn't eat olives."

Thomas nodded graciously.

Like someone bargaining with death, Richard said. "No chicken. "

Thomas looked very sympathetic. "That makes good sense to me, the way they float around in their own urine in the slaughter house."

The two chimed in together, "No cabbage or white vegetables."

Joe was trying to keep a straight face. "I guess that leaves…" He strung out the suspense…"goddam beans."

There was the slightest edge to Thomas' smile. "Just like old times."

Vance started laughing hysterically.

Richard looked alarmed and tried to smile.

With wide-eyed innocence Thomas said, "I hope your expectations aren't too high. I make this interesting pasta with beans and things--.no red meat, chicken, white vegetables, mushrooms, fish or cabbage--what am I forgetting?"

Joe chimed in, "olives!" and began laughing.

When the waitress came to pick up the check, Joe and Richard and Vance ordered another margarita.

Chapter 8

A bird call pierced her inner world, eyes opened on their own…here. She looked around cataloging the strange sights…yes, she was here at Joe's…children's big eyes staring from the picture frames, gray glowing light from the window. She felt the warm cocoon of the covers around her. Another bird answered. She heard the gray hum of distant traffic. Right at this very moment ordinary people from Tucson were starting their routine day absolutely oblivious to this stranger waking up in their midst, a stranger who could do anything that she wanted with this day, better than Christmas morning because she didn't have to count on anybody's gifts, even Joe's…Day One.

Thomas listened for sounds in the house…all quiet… Joe gets up in the afternoon. There was always such a sense of privacy around Joe, radiating like heat from a stove. A vague sense of urgency slowly focused

Thomas' attention on a point in her abdomen, fine-tuning the discomfort...yes, her bladder. Life is so simple. She peeled the warm covers off; a cool Tucson morning soaked into her skin. The stone-cool floor tickled her feet. She mozied on over to the bathroom, sat in the embrace of the toilet seat, and released the pressure in the toilet bowl...rushing like a waterfall... lovely. All the animals on the walls turned toward the source of the clamor. Curiosity satisfied, they nodded their heads kindly; they were mammals too after all. She felt the seat graciously warm underneath--king, or more precisely queen of her realm, no king needed, thank you. Thomas nodded her head with benign majesty.

Processing back to her bed through the cool air she slipped her chilly feet between the sheets warmed by last night's dreams. Then her whole body was enveloped in warm comfort; before she closed his eyes her, she nodded reassuringly at all the sad children...she had plans for the day, but right now some sweet sleep would be...she closed her eyes and smiled.

Her eyes opened to a brighter world...the blue window, birds singing opera, the chorus of traffic. The dreamy sheets around her fell away; she sat up, on the edge of the mattress...neck stretches, body stretches, brushing teeth, stepping into the steaming shower... veil of foggy mystery around her private world of body urges. Little activities almost like prayers she performed each morning. Normally performing these rituals was how she slowly, reluctantly waded into a cold Minnesota morning. This morning she dove into the river, pausing mid-flight just long enough to wander if this is what it's like to be happy.

She picked out clothes to wear; she never admitted to anyone how much time she spent trying to find the right shabby shirt. She did hate combing her hair, each day, more sparse. She also hated cleaning things: floors, windows, vacuuming, dusting, just ask Joe or Danny or any one of those other men with whom she had lived. Now doing dishes was another story; that made sense because she liked to cook even if some of her masterpieces were outlandish. She's a Tom girl...Tom girl, that's funny...yes; she laughed quietly to herself as she even more quietly opened the bedroom door...the sound of Joe softly snoring...what a lovely morning.

She walked through the living room...all the furniture waiting for her. The black cat suddenly scooted from Joe's bedroom, noticed Thomas and froze in terror. Thomas decided to be very, very still. They both stood there motionless. After a few minutes the cat, with supreme wariness, edged through the room past Thomas and fled into the studio; Thomas heard a soft flap of the cat door. Puss barely made a sound as it fled, just like Joe. Thomas remained still in the quiet morning light; the plastic surfaces glimmered... how alive everything seemed to be...everything pulsing, breathing. The simplest deadest object seemed alive in Joe's kingdom...maybe that's the secret he's protecting.

The sound of a car purring by...when Joe and Thomas lived together, Thomas kept trying to change Joe: don't drink so much, don't have affairs, come home in time for supper, talk with me. One morning Joe woke and told Thomas about a terrifying nightmare; someone was cutting the legs off all his furniture, and he was screaming in pain. That's when Thomas began understanding that Joe lived in a world to be left alone. That's when she began wondering whose life she was leading anyway. Thomas softly touched the glimmering coffee table still whispering stories from last night.

Then she sailed slowly into the kitchen. Joe must have dumped out the week old popcorn; the bowl lay belly up like a beached whale by the sink. The morning light pulled Thomas into the studio. There were signs there of Joe's work last night: a different painting on the wall, a can of brushes right under it, an almost empty glass of beer next to the brushes. Thomas moved as softly as Puss; she began melting into the studio. She didn't even move her eyes in an attempt to be still…the only way to take in Joe…yes, Thomas could feel paintings around her. She stilled her breath…there it was, a faint whispering sound. She willed her pulse to a quiet hum: whispering all around her. In her peripheral vision she watched the paintings, layers of colors shifting like oil slicks in the sun, the colorful dreams slowly swirling, folding in on themselves leaving that strange whispering sound behind…a wild place where shapes could never be held on to…no permanence…a Technicolor agreement between the eye and light and time. Normally time begs for meaning and importance, something to be held on to…desire, abhorrence, guilt, punishment, something the hand can seek or hold off…the measure of desire…

the grasping hand passes through the rainbow and is coated with slimy oil, color like time, a fabrication of the imagination, a joke, something to keep the beat going in the background. Thomas examined her own hands…no oil today.

Through the back door she stepped out into the garden, hazy blue morning smelling of ripening grapefruit and the peppery desert: images of her own life, the experiences swirling around, always changing into something else, stubbornly resisting words…a sharp bird call set her body into motion…she did a slow dance of Tai Chi like a wave folding in one herself as yellow globes of grapefruit did their dance of morning ripening. Somewhere in the distance a siren call…the screeching urgency stuck its hand through the swirling morning and everything became an oil slick coating her desperate purposes. So many things she needed to do today; walking back into the kitchen, she studied the clock, each second a discrete movement, each second a tiny concrete place…10:30 AM…things to do. She picked up *Pride and Prejudice* and stepped out of the front door into the universe that thought it was a clock… do universes really think? She pushed the thought aside.

She liked to carry small paperback books in her pocket when he went to eat out alone; she could inhabit new places more easily. It must have sprinkled last night; shallow puddles on the road were steaming, disappearing in the bright morning. She glanced upward beyond her memories, dreams, and even her imagination: towering golden ramparts thrust up all around her, shinning and massive. Her mouth opened in amazement, her eyes trying to piece the impossibility together,:mountains...her feet began moving all on their own, slowly turning her form...her face absorbing the impossibility surrounding her. She had the power to spin mountains around herself and make them dance. Her steps clip clopped in the empty street; her tall floppy form, usually so tentative, dipped and spun in dervish delight, a hymn without words to the Lord of Rings, maybe even Yahweh.

A deep sound from her gut broke the spell. She stopped spinning. Her stomach urgently complained about her lack of focus. Those were only mountains after all, big chunks of stone and earth: mute and dumb. The mystery congealed into hunger. She imagined breakfast.

Walking along the asphalt street winding through the worn quiet suburb...now how does she get to Broadway and the bus? Once she caught the bus, she could get to downtown, from downtown she could walk to the East Side and a restaurant she remembered from her last visit when Joe and Tim lived together. Her stomach twisted impatiently. Her plan...she would follow her plan...she knew the general direction to Broadway and the bus; she could hear the traffic humming...just follow the winding street through the ghost town. The traffic hum was becoming louder, more insistent. Her stomach seemed skeptical, but her feet followed the asphalt curve. Just when she thought that she was caught in a maze, a parking lot came into view. Where there is a parking lot, there is hope of

Broadway. Her pace picked up around the curve…not just any parking lot, but a large one, cars parked like little islands in a sea of asphalt. Towering over that expanse, a chrome and glass building reaching up into the sky, beckoning: Oz. A sign glittered, *"AMERICAN CAFE"*. And there just beyond it flowed Broadway. To confirm her supposition, a bus rumbled along the street. Intrepid Thomas reassured her stomach; her feet no longer following a curved path, shot straight into the parking lot headed to the street beyond.

A car slowly drove into the lot and stopped. The doors opened, in synchrony an older couple, burned golden by the sun stepped out and surveyed the restaurant leisurely. These were people for whom the process of going to breakfast had if not a numinous, at least a significant meaning, people either on vacation or else in the twilight of retirement

when satisfying appetites or responding to urgent bodily needs intruded in the Present at any time. They processed solemnly toward the restaurant, not disturbing the significance of their journey with chatter.

As hardy Thomas briskly journeyed through the lot, she couldn't help but notice or maybe even admire the couple's grace. Perhaps it was just her stomach beginning to create a divergent plan. With some longing she watched the pilgrims open the glass chrome doors and enter the breakfast shrine. Thomas prodded her flagging feet. Passing under the chrome canopy of the restaurant, the rich burnt smell of coffee drew her like a siren call. Her stomach and feet must have come to some sort of resolve. Despite her determined plan, her feet were definitely slowing down, their speed diminishing by halves each moment. Just when she was approaching infinity: that place where time and space melt into each other, her stomach gave out a wail. Her mind castigated her body; she wanted to have breakfast downtown, a real Mexican breakfast, not a chrome plastic facsimile. Her feet stopped; the smell of French toast, greasy and sweet beckoned her. Some traitorous part of herself whispered that she was supposed to meet Joe in a couple of hours and there really wouldn't be time to go downtown. The second hand of a clock slowly melted into butter, yes, she could just picture a rectangle of cool golden butter sitting on a steamy piece of French toast. Slowly, imperceptibly that solid pat was transforming into a fragrant lake that ran across the French toast of her imagination; the promise of golden transformation won the day and turned her feet around.

At first tentatively, then with more speed her feet moved toward the chrome and glass door that opened into an ecstasy of melted butter. Her mind was cutting its losses. After all she was on vacation and she could do whatever she wanted. Smiling, she unfurled her sails and let the force of desire carry her to the stairs; she could feel the wind blowing through her thin hair. Up the two steps covered with all-weather grass like carpet, she could make out all the saints sitting inside the glassed in shrine, lounging in satisfaction. Large shinny chrome letters spelling "*AMERICAN CAFE*" hung over the gate to paradise. She stepped behind another pilgrim, and fell into the procession that filed through the chrome doorway into her heart's desire.

And then breaking through the bonds of delirious expectation, she plunged into that land of attainable promise, a glass enclosed fountain of satisfaction... cheery, sentimental rock and roll invaded her sense...the aroma of fried fat and sweet syrup and dark burnt coffee overwhelmed her...paradise now. She was submerged in the mystery of hushed voices and tinkling silverware, the gates of pleasure opened: American Café. The angels surrounded her, everyone had this fragile eternity to enjoy the delights steaming in front of them. For a moment her own fragile sense of self dissipated as she became one with The American Café. An intense looking middle-aged goddess with a helmet of blond hair piled up on her head approached, her eyes like some Egyptian goddess's were sharp as a hawk's, drawing Thomas forth from his reverie. "Smoking?"

Thomas looked at her directly then glanced away... something about not looking directly into the face of the goddess. She did seem to be in charge here. Was this some sort of test question upon which Thomas' residence in paradise hung? She fidgeted anxiously.

The Goddess' eyes focused on Thomas with threatening majesty.

"Oh I'm so sorry I'm taking up your precious time." Thomas' apology didn't appear to placate the The Goddess's wrath. There was something that Thomas needed to do...the question. She smiled triumphantly. "No."

The Goddess turned away.

Thomas knew she had failed the test...so close to paradise.

"No tables free."

Thomas was grateful for the explanation; goddesses don't need to describe their rationales. Faint hope dawned on Thomas' face. Perhaps this is actually purgatory; after enough anguish she could finally eat French toasts. This hope sparked her powers of observation. She saw an empty chair by the breakfast bar; a possibility was forming in her imagination...no tables...bar. Her face reanimated. Just as The Goddess was about to step away, Thomas said meekly but nevertheless with some determination, "Can I sit here, please?"

The Goddess' departure halted. She turned back to Thomas sternly, maybe even offended. Goddesses are so fragile. "Of course," she waved him toward the counter as if she were swatting a fly.

What if Satan had actually triumphed in *Paradise Lost*? Despite omnipotent divinity, Thomas had achieved her goal. She smiled deviously lowering herself on the shiny swiveling counter chair.

The Goddess disappeared, and Thomas reconnoitered paradise...a relatively clean counter in front of her...that little puddle of coffee doesn't count, menu, she needs some sort of menu to choose from. She looked around surreptitiously. There sitting placidly across the counter was a shiny plastic menu held in a vertical position by an even shinier chrome clamp at the base. Time for action: inconspicuously as possible she reached over to the menu and gave it a tiny little tug. It didn't budge. She glanced around to see if anyone were watching, The Goddess in particular. This might be another one of those tests. She pulled at it a little more insistently; it didn't budge. Perhaps it was fastened to the counter; after all she was traveling and anything was possible. Suddenly her stomach wrenched, complaining loudly. She faced off with the menu. Just when she knew that the menu was gloating contemptuously, her hand flashed across the counter like some striking cobra and gave the menu a sharp, commanding yank. The clamp, surprised and overpowered, released. Triumphantly she gasped; she didn't care who noticed.

She opened the wings of that menu, its arms spreading as if in flight. Gleaming pictures of food filled her eyes: pictures of the Promised Land. For a minute she was overwhelmed by the abundance until her stomach once again complained. She looked at the pages now with resolution…breakfast. There, turning the pages she found it: pictures of French toast. At the very top of the page, "Early Bird Special" greeted her…valid until 10:00 AM. She glanced up at the clock…10:02. She felt an attack of moral ambiguity, transgression beckoned. Normally she was very scrupulous about rules, but today…

An Older Waitress, some sort of demi-goddess perhaps, dark dyed hair, years of serving in heaven having polished her face to a wooden mask of nonchalance; walked toward Thomas. "Coffee?

Devious Thomas looked as innocently as she was able. "Oh yes, do I need a cup of coffee!"

The Waitress didn't seem impressed. "You ready?" She glanced casually at Thomas's opened menu.

Thomas looked away to hide the deceit in her eyes, "I'll have Early Bird Special." She glanced up at The Waitress deviously.

The Waitress stared at him while she scribbled something on a pad of paper.

Thomas hiding behind her innocence, casually said, "I'll have the egg over easy, French toast and sausage." She knew it was essential that she look relaxed. Her body betrayed her…the stool underneath him began turning. To hide the motion she placed *Pride and Prejudice* on the counter.

The Waitress looked oblivious, nodding absentmindedly.

Guilty Thomas opened the book and stared at it numbly. When she glanced back, The Waitress had disappeared into thin air.

That wasn't so bad really. After all she's on vacation. Besides she was getting what she wanted, really wanted… for a change. Catholics say punishment follows sin, the Buddhists say desire is empty. Giddy anticipation welled all the way up from her stomach; she didn't care what they said. She found herself frowning…something's wrong…maybe those religious folks are right. She forgot to order cream! What's a cup of coffee if there's no cream? What's breakfast without coffee? The world is filled with illusions.

Just then in her peripheral vision, she saw a hand push a cup of coffee towards her on the counter. Her determination overcame three thousand years of metaphysics. She jerked her head up quickly, "I'm sorry to bother you, but I'll need some cr…"

The hand nonchalantly pushed a white ceramic bowl full of little plastic creamers closer to her.

Is this forgiveness…maybe even enlightenment? Simple excitement burned off her thoughts as fast as the Tucson sun burned off puddles of waters. The smells of frying sausage and eggs wafted from the nearby grill into her nostrils. Her gut, oblivious to the finer points of metaphysics, took charge. Her hand instinctively picked up a little white plastic creamer. As if by magic both hands opened the container pouring the contents into the coffee. She watched as a white cloud swirled mysteriously in the brown liquid. To speed the color transformation, she picked up a cool stainless steel spoon and stirred the liquid into a homogeneous creamy brown color; she smiled at her ability to participate in mystery. Picking up the thick white handle of the cup (heat from the coffee was already suffusing into the cup handle), she took a little sip. The liquid, just on the pleasant edge of hot, coated her tongue and warmed a path down hers throat. Daring the warmth of the liquid, she took a big swallow. Her whole head felt warm…what an adventure! Heat radiated from her body rippling throughout the restaurant.

Afraid to tempt fate anymore, she turned her attention back to her book. "'In consequence of an

agreement between the sisters, Elizabeth wrote the
next morning to her mother to beg that the carriage
might be sent for them in the course of the day. But
Mrs. Bennet, who had calculated on her daughters
remaining at Netherfield till the following Tuesday,
which would exactly finish Jane's week, could not bring
herself to receive them with pleasure before." Thomas'
nose twitched...a smell...was that a hint of onion? She
looked up from her book. Tentatively she glanced over
the counter. The Waitress must have wiped up the
coffee spill; there beyond the counter, warming lights
cast their golden glow on plates of eggs and pancakes
waiting to be picked up by passing waitresses. Peering
through the steam rising from the plates, she spotted
two men dressed in white, performing a ritual with
spatulas at a hot metal altar. One priest, a Hispanic
looking man with shiny black hair and a matinee idol
face, Rudolph Valentino, gracefully flipped a congealed
mass of scrambled eggs onto a plate. With the spatula
he picked out two crisp brown curls of bacon from a
haystack of bacon on the side of the altar, while the
other hand simultaneously grabbed two pieces of golden
bread from the toaster, swiping them across a block of
sweating yellow butter, throwing them onto the plate
so that the toast rested lovingly between the eggs and
the bacon. Thomas was in love...such aesthetic mastery.
With bravado Rudolph placed his masterpiece under the
golden warm rays of the heat lamp. He turned to the
other priest, also Hispanic, a wispy young man with
dark, large, sad eyes in a narrow face. Both men stood

in a brief moment of reflection, staring at a large pile of hash browns. With measured solemnity Rudolph and the Sad-Eyed Man began flipping that pile over.

Task done, the two celebrants paused, glancing at each, whispering a prayer; returned to their sacrament. They moved in ritualized harmony. At each step of the ritual more plates ended up in the golden heat on the counter. A young pale waitress, maybe a coed, grabbed an armful of plates off the counter. She glanced with enchantment at Rudolph and rushed back to her crowded tables. Rudolph didn't pay any attention to her. That's when Thomas decided that she liked the Sad Eyed Waiter better than Rudolph.

A slim middle-aged waiter who looked like he had been doing this for at least a lifetime picked up several of the plates balancing them with the grace of a ballerina.

A pony-tailed cowgirl of a waitress walked in front of the lamps, examined her pad of orders, and scratched her head.

That is when the ever vigilant Goddess spied The Cow Girl's transgression; those Cow Girl fingers unhygienically scratching her cowgirl scalp. The Goddess swooped down on the Cow Girl; Thomas looked away.

Thomas' own waitress grabbed two plates with nonplussed efficiency, and as she sailed by Thomas, slipped one of the plates onto the counter right next to Thomas' book.

Thomas looked in the direction of The Waitress to express gratitude, but The Waitress was gone. Thomas pushed her book aside, admiring the two white yoked eggs each with promise of marigold softness contained within. A nubbly grayish brown sausage patty, and, yes, above all, French toasts, two golden pieces, brown networks of veins decorating them, sat next to the eggs. On top of each veined slice of French toast, a placid rectangle of yellow butter was beginning to melt into fragrant oil; her feet were on the Promised Land. That look of near ecstasy suddenly shifted into suspicion. Where is the syrup? Just as suspicion was distancing her from paradise, the waitress walked by balancing three plates and somehow slid a bottle of syrup in front of Thomas. She smiled with renewed faith in…not exactly divine providence, but at least faith in The Waitress.

Who cares about Jesus, Buddha and even Jane Austen? Her knife ever so slowly and gently sliced through the pale white skin covering the orange liquid yolk. The thick velvety yellow seeped out of its skin running slowly over the glistening egg white and onto the plate, finally spreading around the brown nubbly sausage patty. She cut the patty in eight equal size pieces and then one at a time dipping each piece into the egg yolk; she slipped each morsel of the sausage into her mouth.

And she hadn't even begun the French toasts. She spread the remaining unmelted butter evenly across each slice, then cut both golden toasts into small triangles, and finally with orgiastic delight poured the thick warm liquid over the careful arrangement. One triangle at a time, she swooshed up the syrup, placing the prize in her mouth. Skilled precision wedded to absolute enjoyment; she cleared her plate. Finally as a tour d'force she speared the last piece of French toast and pushed it lovingly around the entire plate catching syrup and debris…she slipped the piece into her mouth.

The Waitress' arm stretched across Thomas' field of vision presenting her with the check. Thomas' eyes followed up that arm. For the tiniest instant The Waitress looked at Thomas. Maybe it was elevated blood sugar, but Thomas thought The Waitress cracked a smile when she said, "Have a nice day, honey." And then she was gone leaving Thomas basking in the warmth of her affection. She got up from that spinning stool sure that this was a fine day indeed. This could be a new religion.

Chapter 9

When Thomas stepped out of the restaurant, the sky was steely gray, and a chilly wind had snuck in, jabbing at another tanned couple getting out of their car, mussing their clothes. Sharp cold drops of water smacked her face. The tanned couple fled their car, refugees seeking the safety of American Cafe. Her stomach warmed her; the unpredictable weather tickled her fancy. Retracing her steps back to Joe's, Thomas basked in the vindication of her decision not to bus to town. By the time she got to Joe's, raindrops had turned the gray asphalt of the driveway, black. Thomas pushed the door open.

Joe was puttering around in the kitchen drowsily. "Hey." He managed a smile.

Thomas smiled back, "Hey."

"What trouble have you been getting into?" Joe placed one hand on a pale yellow grapefruit sitting on the counter. Drowsily he grabbed a large knife from a wooden stand. The long blade gleamed coolly in the gray light.

Thomas flashed on all the adventures of the morning, her face becoming still...when she was a kid she read about beautiful cave formations, like jewels in Aladdin's cave...she read that as beautiful as they were, when you took them out of the cave they seemed dull and lusterless. Thomas stared at the mustard yellow floor, remembering the smile The Waitress gave her. Finally she said, "I just went to that restaurant on Broadway, the real chromy one. I had a really good time and a waitress there was really nice."

Joe looked at Thomas blankly. He frowned. With an unexpected angry thrust, he slit the grapefruit open. "But when are you going to have fun?"

Thomas looked at the grapefruit halves, oozing watery pink. Her eyes widened watching the knife in Joe's hand. Thomas looked down at the floor...thank goodness the flesh of her morning lay hidden and protected.

Joe grimaced apologetically at the knife. Once again his motions were drowsy. "I can't get a hold of the owner of the gallery. Maybe we should go out later this week. Tim called inviting us for supper tonight." He began squeezing the juice into a glass. The dripping juice sounded like rain...soothing.

Thomas had never been afraid of Joe, except afraid of losing him. Even his sudden bursts of anger directed at nobody in particular seemed more like summer storms. "I'd like to see him. How's he doing, you two being split up and all."

Joe looked down with exaggerated remorse at the mangled grapefruit. "Whore Joe."

"That's not what I mean."

Joe examined the juice in the clear glass. "Jerry will be there."

"Who's Jerry? I'll try not to embarrass you."

Joe gazed out at the gray wet garden. "It's cold!" He glanced at Thomas piteously.

"It is?"

"This is supposed to be sunny Arizona."

You forget where I come from."

He held up the half-filled glass to Thomas. "Want some?"

Thomas shook her head.

Joe took a sip and smacked his lips softly. "What do you want to do this afternoon?"

Thomas looked back, her eyes glazed over to cover the tracks of any desires. "I'm really fine. It'll be exciting to see Tim and I suppose Jerry…an old boyfriend?"

Joe took another sip. He smiled in sly satisfaction. "They're all boyfriends…don't you want to pick up some goodies to eat while you're here? The boys are coming over tomorrow night, and you said you'd cook. " He flashed a teasing smile at Thomas.

"The devil made me do it."

"Pigface."

They studied each other for an instant, then both laughed slyly. Their eyes glanced away at the same time.

Joe took another sip. " I'm headed out to that consignment store. Richard and I have our booth there. I want to check out how much we've sold." He looked embarrassed. "I need to pay the rent."

The glazed look in Thomas' face began clearing away...he had spent years tagging along with Joe... magical mystery tours...an answer to Thomas' dreams of adventure. Joe had this way of taking care of Thomas, but there was always an unexpected drop off leaving Thomas marooned on a shore, older and with a fist full of sand. Thomas, face softening into sadness, watched Joe drinking the grapefruit juice. "That sounds fun."

"The landlord's crazy." That tantalizing smile again...

Thomas warmed. "At least he won't be fashionable."

"Superficial Joe."

"Would you stop that?"

"Let's get going."

Simultaneously the two of them opened the opposite doors to Joe's truck; they used to even walk in step. Thomas shook her head slightly...how could two people who understood each other so little slip into such harmony? She sat on the torn cushion; the musty smell of pee engulfing her...six years ago Joe treated Thomas to a trip down California's Highway One. Thomas was single at that time and teaching in a high school in Minneapolis; Joe was living in Tucson getting ready to separate from Tim. Joe, aware of Thomas' terror of spending money, sent an airplane ticket to Thomas and met him at the San Francisco airport. The first thing that Joe said upon viewing Thomas at the airport was, "Old man." Joe had a way with words.

Thomas, fresh from the horrors of risking his life in a plane, felt his whole body relax as he gave Joe a hug. "I'm so old my ass is dragging."

Joe stepped away and examined Thomas. "Handsome old man."

"Right…nice save."

That funny kind of communion again, as rapid and invisible as the flicker of humming bird wings…then the time clock switched on and they both looked away from each other. From San Francisco they traveled down Highway 1, down the coast in that truck of Joe's that didn't smell of pee yet. They spent the first night in a weird little motel on the edge of a cliff in the Big Sur. Thomas was beginning to wonder if just maybe, maybe Joe wanted her back. Thomas would grumble just a very little and then look tentative, and finally, not take too long to say yes. By the time they unpacked in the chilly motel room, the setting sun had covered itself with a cold numbing fog. They slept in separate clammy beds.

The second night they ended out down coast in a hotel in a town with hot springs. Each room had a sunken bathtub in which at the turn of a rusty faucet, smelly sulphury hot water from deep in the earth would fill the tub. They both sat naked in the hot water and breathed in the rotten egg smelling fumes. Perhaps inspired by the hot bubbling up from deep down in the earth, Thomas decided to put words to his inchoate yearnings. "Do you ever think maybe of getting together again?"

Joe's hand grasped at the faucet. His body seemed to curl up against the side of the grimy tub.

Thomas watched…maybe it was with Joe that she learned about watching.

Joe frantically cranked the faucet to add more water from the deep.

Thomas smiled with sheepish innocence and began talking about teaching school and the weather in Minnesota. His droning voice, mixing with the urgent sound of running water, didn't need a response.

Joe's hand released the faucet.

There were no happy endings with Joe; back then Thomas could still forget that. They reached the end of the line in Los Angeles in a motel on Sunset Strip, free magazines with handsome nearly naked men for rent lay in piles by the telephone. Thomas thought about maybe getting in trouble; Joe kept hoping Thomas would. Around 9 PM, long before any self-respecting gay man would venture out, Thomas decided that he really did like to sleep at night and that getting in trouble was over-rated. And even though he had let go of happy endings, he knew Joe would be leaving the next day and who knows when he would see him again?

It was a sunny hot morning in LA when Thomas woke up. There was something reassuring about the sound of Joe sleeping in the other bed. Thomas gently called out Joe's name to wake him. They dressed with a solemn synchronicity and then stepped into the truck.

The highway was crammed with cars. The momentum with which Thomas and Joe had begun the morning gradually dissipated in the slowing procession of cars on the way to the airport. Sporadically car horns would blare in futile frustration, the whole idea of a destination turning into a delusion. Thomas had made sure that they started early enough, even in the face of infinity... who better to share infinity with?

Joe's face tensed up as tight as a fist.

Thomas noticed and remained silent.

Joe looked over at Thomas. With a look of inconsolable grief he said, "I have to pee."

For an instant Thomas had actually thought that the grief of his immanent departure had something to do with that anguished look on his face.

The car barely inching along was on an elevated freeway. The long line of cars snaking into the horizon suddenly stopped completely. She glanced over at Joe, whose face was clenching tighter by the second. Thomas thought of saying something comforting, but she knew the last thing that Joe needed was distraction. The line of cars began moving again; they two looked at each other with a hint of hope. Thomas even smiled and said, "Here we go." Then the line of cars halted again. This time an entire chorus of car horns coming from all around, blared angrily. The anguish on Joe's face suddenly hardened and then exploded, his hands slapping the wheel viciously. Thomas froze in place, his face flushing in shame; he knew that he was the reason for this situation. Joe could have been relaxing in Tucson drinking a beer if Thomas had only not accepted the invitation. He should have known better.

Joe's face began softening, not with the softness of relief but of despair. He glanced over at his frozen passenger. He sought out Thomas' eyes. Their eyes met in one of those moments of strange communion at the edge of the world. Joe's face tightened ever so slightly in one last fleeting attempt at control. Then as they gazed at each other, Joe's face released in the commotion of blaring car horns. Thomas witnessed the anguished defeat...no plea for sympathy, no excuses...Joe's life emptying into Thomas' eyes. The sour smell of pee filled the warm car. As fast as the flicker of hummingbird wings, the moment was over. The traffic began moving; they glanced at each other in silent apology.

Now, Thomas sat silently in the same truck six years and five hundred miles away from that scene, she wondered again about space and time and how things fold in on each other...certainly not a straight line. She looked toward Joe who was watching her out of the corner of his eye...a ghostly flicker of something.

Joe frowned teasingly at Thomas. "Where were you?"

"In space."

"Pigface is crazy."

"Look who's talking?"

"We'll go pick up groceries first."

"Sounds good to me."

They turned away from each other.

Thomas stared out the side window. Houses were

giving way to small one-story buildings and endless, shabby shopping malls. The car pulled into the parking lot of one of those indistinguishable malls.

As they stepped out of the truck Joe said, "Have you ever been to Hanley's?"

Thomas looked bewildered.

"I bet you don't have them in Minneapolis. Cheap food and wine...you're in for a treat."

"I suppose so."

They stepped into the store, tall canyon walls of boxes engulfing them. Thomas studied those walls more closely. Boxes were open; all sorts of food stuffs and bottles of liquid were spilling out. Young people...to Thomas anyone younger than 40 was young...dressed in fashionably shabby clothes, pushed carts along the aisles greedily grabbing at the piles of food and drink. Joe's face lit up as he stared at all the things crowding around him. He too began piling things into his cart: blueberry juice, cashews, toothpaste, and wine, lots of wine. He glanced over at Thomas who was desperately trying not to knock anything over. It was one of those dangerous places, everything balancing on edge.

Joe grinned. "Get what you want...it's on me."

For an instant Thomas accidentally started to bask in Joe's generosity. She jerked back into reality and almost knocked over a precariously high stack of cans containing olive oil. "I can buy my own food...you've been kind enough."

"Come on...this is my treat. Besides you're feeding

those bums." He grabbed a huge bag of granola that could feed millions. "You like granola."

"Beans…we need beans…okay this once, and next time we come here, it's my turn." With Joe it was always too easy to give in.

Their steps started to synchronize again. Like in a dance they glided through the aisles. Joe watched Thomas pick out Parmesan cheese, pasta, and Italian red wine, and most important two cans of plain pinto beans. Thomas was creating the meal in her imagination.

Thomas looked over at Joe apologetically. "It'll be a real ordinary dinner."

"I don't deserve it."

They both laughed.

Then off to see the crazy man who rented out space in his antique shop to Joe and Richard. The truck drove further out, to the edge of the old town, a place where the wealthier suburban people could wade more easily into urban squalor. They stopped in front of a grungy looking storefront over which hung a large peeling sign on which was written *ANTIQUES*. Thomas followed Joe in…a musty smell of old clothes and something more pungent. A large German Shepard leapt at the two from behind a glass-enclosed enclosure. Joe didn't notice; Thomas backed away to study the situation… the dog was indeed contained by the glass; even more importantly he had begun to wag his tail and smile the way dogs do.

A crazy-eyed man, with a gray ponytail, a raggedy tee shirt with a faded image of Che Gueverra on it, peaked over a large bureau. "Don't mind the dog. Who are you?" He glanced at Thomas without waiting for a response.

He focused on Joe. "Sold a few things."

"I have the rent."

"That turquoise coffee table and the train set."

Thomas stepped closer to Joe. "I'm Thomas."

"And that swan lamp."

Joe laughed. "Richard bet me a dollar we'd never sell that."

The ponytail man scampered over and while addressing Joe, stuck his hand out to Thomas who didn't notice because he was walking over to the smiling dog. "Can I talk to him?"

Ponytail man moved his open hand over to straighten a poodle figurine. "Where are you from?"

Joe handed a check to Ponytail.

Ponytail looked over at Thomas. "Sure, you can pet him."

Thomas glanced up, "Minneapolis."

Ponytail and Joe made eye contact as Ponytail grabbed the check. "It's about time."

Conversation between Joe and Ponytail bounced back and forth without any clear plot line. Thomas started to feel dizzy and stepped away from the two. The store seemed ragged and dusty, filled with things that hardly qualified as antiques. Then she remembered that she was fifty something and what seemed recent to her, seemed ancient to young people. Thomas studied Ponytail...an attractive man about his age, the body settling into curves…how similar men and women start looking when the tide of hormones ebbs…still, like antiques, older people carry history. Very gingerly Thomas began touching things, always unbreakable, securely anchored things. Her fingers could make out echoed vibrations from the ghosts of the past.

The conversation between Joe and Ponytail ended as it began. Both watched Thomas for a moment. Joe said, "Let's blow this joint."

Back home; Joe's day was now over. Night would bring Tim and Jerry and then hours of painting, but before all that, Joe's usual nap.

After the adventure, Thomas lay down in her own bed watching the gray in her bedroom window turning to black. Just as she was trying to identify the exact moment when evening turns into night, she fell asleep.

Thomas woke up. She realized with regret that she had missed that moment when time actually changes… the window looked black. She scratched her head…there was something else she was forgetting. She stared out the black window hoping that she might glimpse whatever she had forgotten. Her eyes opened wide…it's time to call Danny! She hadn't thought about Danny all day. In a flash, space condensed; Tucson and Minneapolis inhabited Thomas' imagination…Joe breathing softly in sleep just in the next room while Danny was telling his stories and jokes.

She blinked away the picture. It wasn't horrible, or maybe she was horrible; she never did know how to make a home for herself, let alone a home for Danny. It was so much easier with Joe; home was wishful thinking. She turned away from the black screen of the window and studied the shadowy faces of the big-eyed sad children peering at her from the walls. Maybe that's how people, Joe too, see Thomas, stylized, looking out at the world with seductive powerlessness. She cautiously and quietly slipped out of bed across the cool floor. She put her hand on one of the framed pictures and very slowly turned it over...no one inside. She stood motionless in the shadowy darkness.

Deep in thought she put the picture back. Flipping on the light switch, she sat on a chair by desk. She picked up her cell phone. No one else knew her cell number, even her, except for Danny. "Hello darling."

Danny sounded happy and then guarded. "How are you doing?"

"Oh, I'm having a good time. I saw two of Joe's friends last night. Everybody smokes marijuana here... oh I suppose not everybody, but it seems pretty common. And then we went out and ate. We talked about some stuff, but mostly I was just getting to know them.

There was silence from the other end of the line. "Is it pretty wild there?"

Thomas caught the worry. "You know me, I hate to get involved. I love you darling"

Danny's voice sounded relieved. "I love you too."

"How have you been?"

Danny's voice picked up momentum. "We had that fund raiser at work. They just don't get it. No one met afterwards to give feedback about the event. That's one of the most basic things about fund raising. They don't know what they're doing. I took Julie aside to tell her about it. I think they think that money just grows on trees."

Thomas nodded benignly; the faces of the big-eyed children filled her imagination. She heard an expectant pause on the other end. She tried to sound empathetic. "Ya."

Danny picked up momentum again. "The meeting with Floyd went alright; I made a list of suggestions and goals. They thought I was the messiah or something."

Thomas tried to remember who Floyd was and then realized that it didn't matter. "You sound like you have a pretty good feel for things there. Be a little careful. When you start a job, people can be pretty touchy about changes."

"I know, I know…I went for coffee with Bill last night."

"How's he doing?"

"Same old, same old, job driving him crazy. He's like a broken record sometimes."

Thomas smiled deviously. "You guys are real buddies."

"I put in a call to Genevieve. She can still talk."

"How's she doing?" Thomas clicked her heels together as if, like Dorothy, she wanted to be back in Minnesota…at least for a few minutes.

"She said I am a good boy."

The two stared out simultaneously as space and time flickered.

Thomas' voice became soft. "You are. When no one saw it, she did."

"And then that was it. I thanked her for everything. She told me to say hello." Danny's voice wavered.

"It's so funny when someone just kind of…I hardly know her but she makes sense…for a few moments, life kind of does too."

Danny started fidgeting in Minneapolis.

Thomas frowned in Tucson one hour earlier.

Flickering present congealed into distance and time.

Danny's voice went fishing for a story. "So it's pretty wild over there."

Thomas crossed her legs. In a placid contained voice Thomas murmured something about everything being all right.

"Did I tell you about Al?"

"Al." Thomas echoed blandly.

"He's started drinking wheat grass juice morning evening and night…he says his hair will turn brown again."

"Really?"

Even 1500 miles away Danny knew he had lost his audience. His voice trailed off.

There was a long pause.

Thomas uncrossed her legs. "Hey darlin' you take care. I gotta go."

Danny's voice sounded disappointed. "Love you…"

"Love you too."

Thomas slowly put the phone down, staring at the black window in the wall opposite her. It wasn't actually the darkness that she feared but the emptiness of that flat surface. A breath from deep down inside Thomas pushed up through her mouth and nose... back again, a cosmonaut returning from space. She blinked her eyes rapidly as if clearing something off her eyeballs...a woman, what does a woman do? She walked back through the studio and into the mysterious garden beyond the window.

Chapter 11

On that second evening in Tucson Joe and Thomas headed off into the night, truck bouncing on the roads as other bouncing headlights shone in their windows.

Thomas glanced over at Joe's face, splashed with the lights of an oncoming car. "I'll try not to embarrass you."

Joe kept looking down the road and then smiled ironically. "Embarrass me? When have you ever embarrassed me?"

Thomas looked deep in thought. "Like when I decided to do yoga during George McGovern's campaign speech."

Half smiling, half moaning, "Pigface...and I'm drunken bum."

The truck pulled up to the side of an old adobe house. For an instant the car lights flashed on a six foot cactus its arms spread in prickly welcome: Tim's place. They stepped out of the jeep, doors banging shut, echoing in the chilly air. Joe pushed through a gate in a stockaded wooden fence.

Thomas stepped through and into another world. Brick paths meandered through bushes and plants that stubbornly refused to stop flowering. Christmas lights hung fiercely from trees and shrubs: a Technicolor apparition on a cold night at Christmas. A small ratty looking terrier charged out of the open back door of the house and eyed the two strangers with fierce indignity.

Joe cooed, "Max…"

The dog looked at him with some misgivings and then began wagging his tale; he edged closer to Joe.

Thomas took a step closer to the pair. The dog, bared his teeth snarling at the intruder.

Joe glanced at Thomas with urgency. "Don't touch him."

Thomas looked apologetic, whispering with exaggerated caution. "Don't worry I won't."

Joe and Max walked toward a bright open doorway; soft orange light filtering into the yard. Thomas followed at a cautious distance. She stepped through the door and into the dining room. A lamp with an orange glowing shade cast light on the soft white adobe walls where hanging masks stared out, some masks fierce and horrifying, others serene and welcoming. An old wooden table stood in the middle of the room; it was set with hand crafted pottery bowls, deep red napkins upon which rested antique silverware. Three candles flickered in the center of the table. The orange light from the lamp glimmered off the-worn-to-a-shine reddish tiles on the floor...chic and rustic all rolled into one ambiance...Tim always did have a way about him, classy, understated. He knew how to make a home.

Tim stepped from the adjoining kitchen to greet his guests. He had put on a little weight since Thomas had seen him last, and the darkness under his eyes added a depth to his face. In the orange light, he looked like a Russian icon staring out at the world. Thomas braced himself.

Tim glanced at Joe and then turned to Thomas.

Thomas saw sadness flicker in Tim's eyes.

Then Tim addressed his guest. "How's Minneapolis?" His voice started off warmly then tightened into irony.

Thomas decided to hug him. "Cold. How are you?"

Tim opened his arms. Their bodies connected with a sudden little shock; they quickly parted.

Jerry walked out of the kitchen...fifty, solid body beginning to soften, native Tucson, massage therapist. He approached Joe with a flirty smile and an edge of disappointment. Thomas could always tell the men that Joe had slept with. Joe and Jerry embraced. Jerry's arms clasped firmly around Joe's waist...just a bit too firmly.

Joe squirmed ever so subtly.

Jerry backed away laughing tensely. "How's tricks?" That disappointed edge again.

Joe looked back at Jerry with mock embarrassment. "I'm a whore." They both laughed.

Joe's confession eased the tension from Jerry's face.

Max moved next to Tim protectively.

"Joe is full of tricks." Tim smiled, the edge of irony again.

Jerry and Tim exchanged a knowing look, Joe the coy focus.

Meanwhile, Max suspiciously eyed Thomas who stood very still, listening to the irony and maybe even broken promises bouncing back and forth between the three…she never did really understand the violence of irony, let alone sarcasm; it seemed so dangerous to her…a long, long time ago in adolescence when she finally understood that she didn't believe in god, she kept trying to figure how to distinguish right and wrong. One evening walking around in the dusk, it came to her…her moral imperative: never try to punish anyone she had loved. Back then it was a start and even now….

Joe said, "Jerry do you remember my friend Thomas?"

Jerry looked over at Thomas, surprised that someone else was in the room.

Thomas knew it was time for him to look warm and inoffensive.

"Yes."

"It's so nice to see you again."

Tim pushed the conversation to the side. "How about some wine? White or red?"

Joe smiled benignly at Thomas. "I took Thomas to Hadley's…cheap wine."

Tim corrected Joe. "Not cheap, inexpensive."

Joe stared straight at the bottles on the table and said with teasing defiance. "It's cheap...cheap!"

Jerry watched the two, "Now boys..."

All three laughed, but there was a little edge, at least that's what Thomas heard. "I'll have some red. It really was a bargain. What a great store!" Thomas stepped away from the trio and poured herself a glass of wine. She really did like red wine; it tasted so deep...she felt the taste in her mouth and the warmth of it going down...even better she knew there would follow a kind of warm fuzziness...she could fade leaving her more time to listen and watch. She felt the smooth bowel of the glass as she took a step back over to the others... yes red wine is so nice. She joined their circle, but kept one foot out behind, either to brace herself or to flee. Nodding, she hardly listened to the conversation not meant for her, loving her private identity, transgender. She could listen and even be there, but also watch these people that really were different from her. She wasn't exactly sure where the difference lay, but she could feel it.

Joe poured himself a glass of white wine.

Jerry perked up. "How about a smoke?"

Tim squinted with comic disapproval at Jerry. "Oh no here he goes again...days of wine and roses.'

Joe looked up from his wine, "Sure."

"Well, I suppose I could have some." Tim murmured.

Thomas thought about it a little...she really did like the feeling after smoking and she was separate really...it would be all right. She smiled genially, "That sounds fun." The ritual of papers and marijuana and rolling and fire began. Thomas watched the faces of the three behind the smoke, not unfriendly faces, but speaking a language she didn't really understand. Of course she understood them enough to respond genially; a ghost, that's what she was. She nodded at nothing in particular…it's not so frightening to be a ghost. She was surprised when Jerry handed her the glowing joint… maybe only half a ghost. She smiled, clasping the joint, nodding benignly, she took a shallow puff and then exhaled, her face veiled with smoke and safety. Her fingers and toes came to life…if she is a ghost, then ghosts feel. Ghosts are alive, but they just can't be seen as easily as other people…there's this part of ghosts that doesn't bounce around but nestles somewhere inside… not just because it's safer there, but because inside is a good place to be…ghosts can watch and let things become…how strange. She nodded to know one in particular.

Thomas watched a large white cat pad softly with heartbreaking grace into the room: another ghost. The cat looked around casually, not searching for approval, simply coming in to see what was going on. Max watched it suspiciously; he could see ghosts. The cat paused, glanced at Max and sidled against Joe's chair. Joe noticed the ghost and smiled; his hand dropped down to touch the arched furry back. "Kitty."

The cat looked up and answered in a high-pitched little melody and walked with phantom grace out of the dining room into the living room.

Tim stood up from the table. "How about supper?"

Joe meowed, "Dindin."

Thomas lifted her veil. "Can I help you?"

Tim looked at her kindly, no edge of irony. "Everything is set; I'll bring it out."

The veil slipped back over Thomas' face as she nodded benignly.

Tim disappeared for a moment and then reappeared holding a plate of golden corn bread. He disappeared again and then came back with dark iron pot out of which stuck a ladle. He set the pot in the middle of the table and sat down. He looked at Thomas, "Can I serve you?"

Even though Thomas was learning to enjoy being a ghost, she looked at Tim and with a purring tone and whispered, "Oh yes." She offered his bowl up to her host.

Sacramentally Tim ladled beans and big chunks of ham into the bowl. As he handed it back to Thomas, he looked over at Jerry who handed him his bowl.

Jerry raised his eyebrows in mock horror. "I heard that Mike Anderson was in town."

Tim cooed as he ladled the stew into Jerry's bowl. "Just when I thought it was safe to go in the water again."

Thomas watched the others laugh.

Jerry looked over at Thomas. "Do you know Mike?"

Tim handing the bowl back to Jerry glanced at Joe, "Your turn."

Joe nodded noncommittally.

Thomas said, "Yes." She scratched her head. Was this some kind of drug flashback?

Tim ladled beans into Joe's bowl. "Mike Anderson,

now there's a real treat." He shook his head in exasperation.

Jerry nodded. "Now there's a mess."

Thomas watched them. "He's a wizard."

No one heard her.

Tim nodded at Thomas.

Maybe Tim did hear her.

Tim looked knowingly at Joe and Jerry and then glanced at Thomas. He ought to meet Ralph."

Thomas watched the other three laugh.

Jerry shook his head. "They even sound alike."

Tim grinned. "They do."

Humor tightened into condescension.

Thomas felt it, but when you're a ghost things like condescension don't matter as much. "Who is Ralph?"

The three sobered up, dropping the sarcasm. Joe said, "He's a very nice man who has a baby with two lesbians."

Tim looked straight at Thomas; he seemed apologetic. "You both use some of the same words."

Thomas smiled warmly as if that were a compliment.

Tim looked down.

"I really would like to meet him." Thomas looked over at Joe.

Joe looked pleased. 'I'll call…we'll get together."

The three silently ate their stew. Joe started fitfully separating the ham from the beans. He looked piteously at Tim. "We lived together for ten years and you still don't know I hate ham."

Tim looked mortified, but was that a faint flicker of satisfaction on his face?

Jerry looked over at Thomas. "Have you met THE COUPLE?"

Thomas looked bewildered...couple...the pieces of his memory came together. "You mean Richard and Vance?"

Tim and Jerry eyed each other.

Joe continued pushing pieces of ham to the side of his bowel.

Jerry grinned, "The dynamic duo."

"They seem pretty nice...they sure do like 60's furniture." Thomas took a large piece of the corn bread. That would go nicely with the ham and beans...so nice to be able to be a ghost.

Tim watched Joe separating the ham out, righteousness mounting.

Joe looked up piteously again. "Nobody remembers about me."

Thomas shook his head slightly...funny how Joe attracts adulation and anger.

Tim disappeared into the kitchen for a few minutes and finally came out holding a beautiful key lime pie; baked egg white like a white mountain range on top. The other three examined it in awe.

Joe lit up. "My favorite!"

Tim smiled in vindication.

Jerry then disappeared into the kitchen bringing out a pot of coffee.

Food and drink finished, conversation winding

down to a halt; Tim directed them into the living room. The cat was waiting for them on the sofa. There was a fire burning in the ancient fireplace, a large irregular polished piece of dark wood resting on short legs crouched between the fire and the sofa. Two big stuffed chairs enclosed the ends of the sitting space. A piece of Joe's art, a quadrant with different colors hung on one wall. The three sat down placing their drinks on the table; Joe and Jerry sat by the cat on the sofa. Thomas and Tim inhabited each a chair; Max sat on the floor next to Tim, guarding.

Thomas settled in, contentedly nested in the chair, a good vantage point for watching. "That's a lovely table. It looks so old and unusual." He really did like it; it looked alive in the glimmer of the fire, and so touchable.

The statement just sat there for a few moments, flickering by the fire.

Tim finally rose to the occasion, explaining that the table was actually a Nigerian bed.

Thomas stared at the object as it slowly transformed from a table to a bed. She nodded in amazement at the transformation, "Yes."

Just then the cat stirred on the sofa, stretching luxuriously. Casually it slipped to the floor, heading for Tim. Faster than the eye could see, Max, who could see ghosts, lunged viciously at the cat, both were transformed into a spinning circle of rage and terror, round and round blurring. The wheel spun so fast it seemed to disappear like vicious hummingbird wings. Teeth bared and growling like thunder, Max paused watching his prey. The cat, electrified with terror glared at Max. The four people watched in horror, motionless, the tragedy transfixing them. As if sparked by a sudden powerful electrical jolt the cat leapt high into the air screaming and clawing at Max's head. The dog dodged howling as the cat flew over him like some Kung Fu fighter and disappeared into a back room. Once more emboldened, the dog followed in savage pursuit. Screams and growls and crashes exploded in the back room.

All this happened in seconds; Tim was the first to mobilize. He frantically ran to the back room screaming Max's name. The other three sat frozen in shock: silence now in the back room.

Thomas sat there, pale, feeling the terror like some recurrent theme repeating in her heart. She waited to see Tim step back into the room with the bloody corpse of the cat.

Joe looked down in shame as if somehow this were his fault.

Jerry kept glancing at Joe for reassurance.

The sound of Tim's slow footsteps came closer. He entered the room, pale as a ghost.

The other three watched him sit down in silence.

Some of the usual irony seeped back into Tim's face. "Puspus is no worse for wear. He's sitting up in the closet."

Max pranced into the room and once again stationed himself by Tim.

Jerry tried unsuccessfully to look reassured.

For an instant Tim looked up at Joe like a lost child.

Then a usual ironic smile covered any vulnerability. The room snapped back to normal.

Thomas watched.

The cat was out of the bag.

Chapter 12

· ·

That second morning in Tucson, Thomas awakening…a screaming cat tore through her imagination. Staring up at the ceiling, a memory hovered above her head…when she was a child, she had been terrified of ghosts for years and years…one morning in late adolescence she realized that her fear of ghosts had been transmuted into fear of the future. At that time she felt an uneasy sense of accomplishment for having become aware of this new reincarnation. Now as she stared at the ceiling she knew that the next reincarnation of fear was old age, pain and death. She turned her head to study the portraits of the big-eyed children. Perhaps that hint of satisfaction in their eyes wasn't coyness after all, just relief at still being alive, and who knows what might happen next…strange how much she liked to wake up with Joe sleeping nearby, over there in the next room, not at the center of her life. Thomas had survived Joe…a different kind of reincarnation began emerging…certainly not hope or satisfaction, but some increasing awareness, perhaps a pearl beyond price. Birds were singing and once again the window shone blue; she would take the bus today. Quietly finishing all her morning rituals, some rituals even surviving reincarnations, she stepped out of the house, locked the door behind herself, and set off through those empty suburban streets in the deserted ghost town, the sky, a blue crystal. There like a surprise birthday party the mountain giants stuck their heads up all around her again…she used to have nightmares about wondering empty war-torn streets; in this Tucson reincarnation she luxuriated in the privacy of the empty streets. Her stomach woke her up from reverie…the smell of French toast filled her imagination…yes, she would go to that restaurant again…so many lovely choices when you're alone.

She stepped through the chrome and glass door, back into the 60's. It was quiet today, Monday morning; a few pairs of people sat at the tables eating and whispering confidences to each other. The severe Goddess from yesterday glanced at Thomas and nodded towards the counter, perhaps a little dismissively the way goddess do sometimes. Thomas sat down carefully on the swiveling stool and gave the menu a sharp yank; it came out with a sudden jerk…lovely. Just as Thomas was opening the menu, The Older Waitress stuck a cup of coffee and a container of cream in front of her and said, "Same?"

Thomas caught the meaning right away and smiled as if greeting an old friend. "Sure."

The Older Waitress disappeared.

Sitting on the stool Thomas realized that she had forgotten to bring *Pride and Prejudice,* and glanced around uneasily...naked without a book. Rudolph Valentino waved his spatula in the air blessing the restaurant. The Sad-Eyed Cook laughed like a sly altar boy as he placed a plate of pancakes under the golden light. The Goddess fiercely honed in on the young Cowgirl Waitress again. She had been scratching her cowgirl scalp again. Suddenly she knew that she was being watched and started anxiously skittering from table to table. The Goddess, now a great bird of prey, circled above the Cowgirl, watching, closing in, getting ready to pounce. The Cowgirl's head bent down, exposing the back of her neck to attack, presenting herself as sacrifice to the fierce deity. The Goddess pointed a deadly talon at the Cowgirl...there, the point of impact. The Cowgirl's whole body went limp, playing dead as the predator raked over her. For an infinity of shame The Cowgirl and The Hostess congealed into a frozen tableau... silence. Then Tthe Cowgirl's neck straitened ever so slightly as she glanced sideways at the restaurant... people were continuing to eat, casually as if something terrible had not just happened. The Goddess also looked out over the restaurant, surprised at her surroundings or maybe just afraid to be seen as a predator. The Cowgirl began nodding, nodding, nodding. The Goddess now smiled with benign satisfaction. The Cowgirl felt that smile and scurried away like some mouse whose life had just been spared, surviving another reincarnation of fear.

Just thenTthe Older Waitress slid breakfast in front of Thomas. Though her salivary glands were pumping full force, she couldn't stop thinking about the Cowgirl. She had so many things she wanted to share with the Cowgirl…maybe to tell her that sometimes things get hard, even terrible and that it's not her fault that she's frightened. The Cowgirl now was frantically taking an order at a faraway table. Thomas turned away.

Besides the sausage was browned, the eggs slithery, and the French toast…the outside all crusty, but the insides soft like custard…appetites are lovely…maybe. Her whole self concentrated on the pleasure of her breakfast.

She cleaned the last bit of egg yellow up with a last bit of syrupy French toast. The Older Waitress nonchalantly came by, placed the check next to Thomas' her plate, looked her in the eye for a flicker of a second, and said, "Have a nice day, honey."

Thomas broke into a smile. "Oh thank you, I sure hope that you have a nice day too."

This Older Waitress nodded before disappearing.

The impact of the words and nod of The Older Waitress rippled through Thomas. Fueled for her adventure, she stepped out of the 1960's and back to the present. The traffic moved along Broadway as if on a noisy conveyor belt…thank goodness for stop lights. She stood on the busy corner…red light…she glanced down the road to see if a bus was coming…she hated to just barely miss a bus. The light turned green; there across the street, on the corner that she approached, sat a strange kind of house, just like one of those other 60's houses in Joe's neighborhood except it stood all alone on a busy corner, no houses on either side. Christmas lights outlined a somber wooden crucifix planted in the front yard right in front of the picture window which had some sort of colored transparent plastic on the inside to make the window look like stained glass. Thomas admired the desperate ingenuity and then noticed a bench by the bus stop.

She sat on the bench in the sun, her back to the mountains, but she could still feel them. An Innocent Faced Woman walked up to the bench and stood next to Thomas. Half in anxiety and half just wanting to talk to her, Thomas said, "Does this bus go downtown?"

Taken by surprise, The Innocent Faced Woman studied Thomas intently. Her face slowly released into the pleasure of confidentiality. "It comes real often."

"Oh good, I'm new around here."

"Where do you come from?" She spoke slowly as if grasping for each word.

"I come from Minneapolis, Minnesota. That's far north and very cold. Thomas spoke even slower than usual. "Are you from here?"

"Here?" Bewildered, she looked down the street. A bus was coming. More confidently she said. "You can catch the bus right here."

"Thank you."

The Innocent Faced Woman nodded protectively at Thomas as the accordion doors opened.

Thomas sat midway down the almost empty bus. The Innocent Faced Woman sat right behind the bus driver. The two seemed glad to see one another and talked on and off during the trip. A Young Black Woman in the back of the bus was playing some kind of computer game; occasionally chiming bells would ring from the little game box. A Hispanic Looking Man dressed in a shabby nurse's uniform sat staring out the window. Two young boys right behind Thomas talked to each other in high voices punctuated by bursts of laughter. All the time the windows shone of blue sky as buildings sailed along. Thomas, staring intensely out the window, was trying to memorize landmarks so she knew when to get off the bus when she was returning. For this trip though, Joe said that Thomas simply needed to go to the end of the line. The end of the line sounded like such a definite inevitable destination, and Thomas knew that inevitability was immune to mistakes, or at least almost.

The two boys got off near a large school. The Innocent Faced Woman said goodbye to the bus driver who said that he would see her tomorrow. The Young Black Woman in back stopped playing the game or turned down the sound...the end of the line... it was unmistakable. The bus driver pulled into an open air terminal and turned the engine off

The main street by the terminal looked like it had seen better days...empty store windows, not much foot traffic…now what is the name of that street that she had visited the last time she was here…when she was a he…the street with all the old hippy shops? Fourth St., that's it. She stood on the sidewalk; streets angled out in different directions, a puzzle, just a puzzle. She had last been in town six years ago; Joe gave Thomas a tour…yes it was Fourth St. Like a puzzle she studied the pieces of her memory, a game, not like fleeing from some vague menace in a confusing and deserted city.

She chose a random direction and walked along the sidewalk; when it's a game it's easier to notice things. She watched her reflection move along the glass storefront windows. Her reflection now a stranger, a drooping middle aged man on the brink of being elderly. What a puzzle, not disturbing really. She kind of liked that middle aged body that she inhabited; besides she was used to things not fitting. The middle aged reflection stopped in front of a glass door over which a fancy wrought iron canopy hung. Thomas stepped up to the door and peered in, a cavernous lobby, marble floors, she put her hands up to the side of her face to shade her vision, a desk sat in the hall with a woman behind it dressed in some fancy kind of uniform, yes, a hotel, a fancy old hotel. Thomas put her hands back to her sides. What business did she have intruding on so solemn a space? She wanted to turn away but the middle aged man's feet remained stationary. She stared at him: her reflected companion. They were both on vacation; they can do anything they want. Their hand reached for the door and gave it a gentle but definite push. Open-says-me, she walked through the doorway and into another world.

The sound of her footsteps on marble echoed as her eyes became accustomed to the dimness of the cavern, the high ceiling arching above her. Her feet moved toward The Charming Clerk behind the desk. A Handsome Man with a German accent was asking her directions. She seemed so professional but still charming. Thomas stepped into an imaginary line behind The Handsome Man. The Charming Clerk pulled out a map and traced a line on it; she looked up at the Handsome Man very graciously. He glanced up at her gratefully, thanked her and left. Thomas walked up to the desk. "Could you tell me how much rooms are for rent? A friend of mine might want to come here some time."

The Charming Clerk looked down at Thomas' dusty shoes and then flashed a charming smile. "Our rates change with the season."

Thomas felt the smile and looked up nodding with gratitude. "It's so nice when things change like that. There's always surprises."

Her face tightened as she studied Thomas.

Thomas nodded more urgently.

With renewed and slightly strained charm The Clerk smiled and graciously picked up a brochure on the edge of the counter, her hand extending out to bestow the brochure. "This describes the hotel, services and rates."

Thomas looked tentative.

She nodded. "You can take it."

Thomas smiled gratefully took the present. "It's a very pretty lobby."

The Charming Clerk paused and looked around with a tiny sense of innocent wonder as if she had never seen her surroundings before. She metamorphosed back into an official self. "Thank you. I hope that you will be a guest here someday."

Thomas beamed at her and started to step away... maybe sometime Danny and she would come...Danny liked to stay in hotels instead of at people's houses. Thomas froze in her steps. She turned around abruptly with an anxious look on her face. Again she moved in front of The Charming Clerk who was preoccupied with urgent calculations. Thomas cleared her throat apologetically. "I'm so sorry to bother you again."

The Charming Clerk's face tightened in irritation; she finished one last computation and then looked up, her face transforming into a charming mask.

Thomas was curious about those transformations... somehow she felt a little closer to the mystery of time... if only the hummingbirds would...

"Can I help you with something?"

"I was so busy thinking that my partner might like to come here that I forgot to ask directions."

She looked at Thomas a bit bewildered.

"Do you know how I can get to Fourth St?"

She look relieved and pulled out a street map from a pile of street maps, opened it and traced out a path with the pen with which she had been computing. "Just take a left and then another left right by the Greyhound bus station. You'll see an underpass. Just follow that."

Thomas studied the map intensely and then half turned to the glass doors opening to the street. "That way?" She pointed to her left.

"That's it." The Charming Clerk nodded her head a little too emphatically.

Thomas smiled at her with overwhelming gratitude.

She was on her way, Fourth St, a sort of left over from the 60's, a musty smelling second hand bookstore presided over by a man sitting in a big pile of books reading, only glancing up as a new person entered the shop, his face nested in wild gray hair, and a food coop… she needed to make supper tonight maybe she'll be inspired there…food often inspired her…those strange transformations…her steps slowed…sun and water and earth and air…then living plants transformed by death into food, and then…the Greyhound station slowly floated into view. Despite the Technicolor mural on the wall, the station sat there at the corner looking abandoned and desolate…something about bus stations and lonely people…now where's the underpass? She stopped on the empty sidewalk in front of the lonely station and turned left…so far so good. She noticed a tunnel going under railway tracks, yes an underpass. She studied it. The sidewalk and the road disappeared into the ground like a passageway to the underworld, like the past. She carefully looked both ways and crossed the street to the entrance of the tunnel. Yes, when she looked down into the tunnel the smell of stale urine brought pictures and feelings from six years ago…that presumes the sequence of time…she stopped halfway through the tunnel…now if time and space are indeed fictions, what had just happened? Was her experience in Tucson six years ago hovering just beyond her sight, just waiting to peek at her from the shadows? She studied the messages scrawled on the dark crumbly walls, desperate messages of anger. If she looked very carefully she could just catch the shadows of the hands that had posted their messages to the world.

The sound of wheels churning rapidly in gravel closed in on her. Startled, she turned around to see a man even older than herself speed by on a rusty old bike…Thomas felt the wave of air rush by her. She watched the man disappear into the light at the end of the tunnel…things sneak up out of nowhere and then disappear again, like the pathways marked in cloud chambers. Her fast beating heart was all that was left of the stranger.

The pathway through the tunnel started rising towards the brilliant exit…follow the light, and presto a slightly different person emerged out of the tunnel into the bright day. This different person looked out over the land that she had discovered…people walking on the streets…a stray dog…yes, this is Fourth St.

A Young Man with a weather worn face and scared eyes approached Thomas. The Young Man trying hard to look meek, put his hand out in front of Thomas' face. "I'm trying to get to Phoenix; my car broke down and I

don't have any money. Please help me. Any amount…."
His voice trailed off in supplication.

Thomas' heart was just slowing down after her
adventure in the tunnel; she looked away from those
begging eyes to study a crumpled piece of paper in
the gutter…years ago she had heard a man talking on
television who had lived as a street person…he said
that the hardest part for him was that no one would
look at him…he was hungry and broke, but what was
even worse; no one saw him…he was invisible, maybe
even a ghost…a ghost. Now Thomas knew that she
really wasn't particularly kind. She was too afraid, but
she could at least let this young man know that she,
Thomas, saw him. Thomas' head turned away from the
crumpled piece of paper and meekly focused on The
Young Man. "I really don't have much money." There,
she made eye contact. The young man's eyes were as
blue as the desert sky, and his face especially around the
eyes was covered with little weather beaten wrinkles…
butterfly wings.

The Young Man looked disappointed; his voice
trembled with demanding need. "I just need a few
dollars for a bite to eat." His outstretched hand was
shaking.

Thomas felt ashamed and then just wanted to be
somewhere else; her gaze wavered.

"Just a few dollars would help me out." Those blue
eyes were burning through Thomas.

What would a woman do? Thomas looked away
again…she's not a saint by any means and she doesn't

really want to be a martyr…but she doesn't want to just pretend to be somewhere else. Her hand unconsciously went to the pocket holding her change. She felt the smooth warm metal surfaces; they jingled. She looked straight at those desert eyes. "I have change."

The Young Man started shaking his head.

"This is for you." Thomas handed him a handful of change.

Still shaking his head The Young Man grabbed the coins from her hand and fled.

Thomas was left with her palm open, the memory of The Young Man's hand still warm and dry on her skin.

Thomas walked on in search of the bookstore and its resident hippy…so many new souvenir shops almost all with the same little objects…no sign anywhere of the old book shop. She did see a new looking store…a bookstore up ahead. "THE WOMEN'S PRESS, she gazed in the window to see two handsome looking women one with short gray hair and the other with long wavy brown hair. Thomas paused studying her own gray haired male reflection on the window superimposed over the women inside…she was intrigued by puzzles.

She stepped into the shop avoiding eye contact with the two women…row upon row of books…women's biographies…women's health…women's recovery… woman's meditation books. She got lost looking at the titles in this woman's world.

"Can I help you with something?".

She jumped.

The Wavy Brown Haired Woman looked as startled as Thomas did. "I didn't mean to scare you."

So many adventures today...Thomas caught her breath. "I'm just easily startled...you're fine."

They smiled tentatively at each other.

The Wavy Brown Haired woman took charge. "Are you looking for anything special? Maybe I can help you."

Thomas looked away. She was just about to shake her head and slink away when she thought, what would a woman do? She paused. "I was actually looking for an old used book store I saw here years ago."

The woman looked at her kindly. "That was a while back." She looked thoughtful. "I think it's a souvenir shop now."

Thomas nodded her head. "I guess things change."

"They sure do."

Thomas scratched her beard deep in thought. "I've been reading *Pride and Prejudice* for the millionth time..."

The Wavy Brown Haired Woman smiled. "It's a truth universally acknowledged that a single man in possession of a good fortune must be in want of a wife."

They both started laughing.

Thomas glanced over at her. "You too?"

"I was crazy about Jane Austen. I still am, but I read other books now. Do you know that she never was married? She died in her forties."

Thomas listened stunned, "Do you mean she never found Darcy?"

"Nope."

"But she writes like she knows all about it; I mean falling in love and marriage."

"Did you ever find Darcy?"

Thomas looked away. She shook her head hesitantly.

The Wavy Brown Haired Woman watched Thomas, her face softening. "I love her imagination, but I'm not Elizabeth Bennet. Nobody is. We're just ourselves."

Thomas slowly turned her head to make eye contact with her. "Did you ever want to be somebody else?"

She looked through Thomas as if she were studying something far away. She smiled to herself. "I spent years living other people's stories."

"You too?" Thomas looked relieved.

"I still like books." Her arm waved with majestic irony at all the shelves of books around them.

Thomas' eyes steadied, resting on her new friend. "I'm glad you're doing something that is kind of connected to what you used to do. Sometimes I think I need to be absolutely different than the mess I made of my life."

"Mess?" The Wavy Brown Haired Woman studied Thomas' face with amusement.

For one second Thomas felt embarrassed, but the innocence of The Wavy Brown Haired Woman's eyes tickled him. Before Thomas knew it, she was laughing.

And then they both were, pitching into an avalanche of laughter.

Just then another person entered the shop. The Thomas and The Wavy Brown Haired woman glanced in that direction.

"Life calls."

Thomas nodded reassuringly to The Wavy Brown Haired Woman as she moved towards the customer.

"Can I help you with anything?".

Thomas watched and said to no one in particular. "Thanks so much." And she meant it.

She stepped out of the store, on her way again. Now, there was something else she wanted to do… supper…food…coop. She stopped on the sidewalk, her eyes searching up and down the street, searching for a ghostly memory. There, a block away, on the corner, with a large wooden sign over it: "COOP." Was she in a time machine? Her feet didn't care and moved with increasing velocity toward that remembered sign and store…there is some sort of continuity in the universe, although Thomas suspected that it wasn't time as we know it. Yes, she was making supper tonight for guests, and the Coop was the perfect place to get those last minute things..

Chapter 13

Pasta y fagiole...not fancy, Monday night fare...
she said it would be simple, besides Vance doesn't
eat fish, neither of them eat red meat...and there's
something else he doesn't eat...mushrooms. Thomas
loved to smash garlic, the aroma exploding in front of
her, then chopping it and as a climax throwing it into
the hot oil...sizzling...as the garlic turns golden brown,
nutty perfume fills the kitchen. She didn't want to
embarrass Joe with pretensions of being a good cook,
or did she? Pretense was for dating. But still she liked to
cook: the colors of things and the way smells mix, the
textures. She could hear the sound of the knife slicing
through the living sacrificial tomato. And cooking
with wine and Italian parsley...flat leaves roughly cut,
thrown in at the end to cook just long enough to make
everything taste like a summer day...besides if they
didn't like her cooking...

Joe stepped into the kitchen still looking drowsy after his nap. "Mama mia."

"It's just going to be ordinary." Thomas held up a romaine lettuce leaf to the light of the sun...translucent green. With poignant tenderness she tore the leaf into small pieces. Was that translucent tearing sound pain or pleasure...plants are so very strange.

"I talked to Ralph."

Thomas looked puzzled...so many names; she put the cooked beans into the sizzling pan of oil and garlic.

"You know, Ralph, the guy who lives with the baby and lesbians."

Thomas nodded.

He'd like to meet you. How does tomorrow night sound?"

"What's Ralph like?"

Joe smiled coyly at Thomas. "Do you mean what does he look like?"

"I suppose sort of...I don't know." Thomas mashed and stirred the beans ferociously.

"He's a very nice man, and he looks all right."

"I don't want it to be like a date or anything." The beans and the liquid began to erupt, bubbling up, bursting, and releasing steam...like mushy valves. Whenever things got too close or too complicated in a relationship, Thomas would go off into romantic fantasies...a pressure valve, an escape...even when she was with Joe. She could always escape into her dreams, those ghostly flickers...she whisked olive oil and lemon juice together and then glanced back at Joe.

Joe had that knowing cynical look on his face; the all-you-need-is-a-good-fuck-look.

Thomas had hated that look; he used to believe it. Now she was a woman; women aren't defined by men…no need to argue or defend…she was her own person. Shaking her head and she went back to stirring the beans.

Joe shuffled out of the room.

Let's see… the salad's ready, romaine lettuce and ripe tomatoes…a vinaigrette dressing…at least sort of. She turned the beans way down; she would wait until Richard and Vance came to put the pasta in…of course fresh parsley. She heard Joe in the dining room setting the table.

Joe walked back into the kitchen and pulled out a few colored enameled bowels. Stepping back, he studied them as if they were part of a painting. He turned toward Thomas confidentially. "What do you think of these colors?"

Thomas turned around, staring at the bowls reflectively. "Ya, I like the combination." I'll need one for the pasta and one for the salad. These two maybe." She pointed to two bowels.

There was a rhythm going on between them. Joe picked up the biggest bowel. "And this one's for potato chips."

"That's swell."

The doorbell rang. They looked at each other, frightened.

Joe melted into his sad-sack self. "Bum house."

Thomas' face smoothed over into an approximation of calm; only her eyes looked tense. She turned back to the stove resting her hand on the on the handle of the pan...Vance's thick shoulders flashed across her mind... the dinner will be stupid...she saw herself, an absurd looking older man who thinks she's a woman...sideshow time...living other people's stories...she picked up the wooden spoon resting on the counter top and gave the beans a reassuring stir. She heard Joe's steps scurrying to the door...the sound of the door opening.

Joe's voice sounded casual, even a little coy. "Look whose here?"

Richard's voice played along. "Who were you expecting, some hunky plumber ready to clean your drain?"

Thomas tried to disappear into the kitchen, eyes closed. She opened her eyes as she took a deep breath and went out to face the music. Her pace was slow, her expression, benign somnolence.

"So glad you could come." At least that's what Thomas thought she said and gave Richard a quick hug.

Richard hugged back as if this weren't a formality. "Wouldn't miss it for the world."

Joe looked at them in satisfaction.

Thomas noticed Vance hanging back a little, still on the front stoop, standing back like some afterthought, looking like some high school dream, all boyish with fullback shoulders covered by some sort of high school jock jacket, and of course the baseball hat on backwards.

Thomas glanced up at Vance slyly. "And how are you?"

Vance shrugged the way boys do when they're trying desperately to look cool.

Thomas tried her best Elizabeth Bennet impersonation...discrete yet direct with just a hint of archness. "Did you work today?"

Joe took Vance's jacket.

Vance looked panicked for a second and then his face covered over with the appearance of indifference. With some effort he opened his mouth. "I told Mary to arrange the discs in alphabetical order. I come back an hour later and she'd arranged them alphabetically by title instead of artist." His voice was high and taught, stretched by tension and complaint. He laughed in strange little punches as he glanced at Richard.

Richard laughed in forced sympathy. "Vance works in Shroeder's music department on Broadway."

Vance continued with his moving train of thought. "I said to her, what planet are you from anyway?"

Joe teased. "You're not getting in trouble again are you?"

Everyone stopped laughing and there was frozen silence. Thomas broke the ice. "How long have you worked there?"

"Too long." Vance tried to sound cavalier.

Presiding Joe said, "How about a beer."

Richard pulled a bottle of vodka out of a brown paper bag. "Grapefruit season!"

Joe caught the wave, "Harvey Wallbangers! I'll go out and pick some."

They both left the room. Vance stepped into the living room.

Thomas smiled at him graciously. "I'm so glad you could come." She motioned to the sofa...be gracious now, this is the Nineteenth Century.

They both sat down at least two feet away from each other.

Thomas waited for some sign of warmth from Vance...silence except for the sound of Joe and Richard in the kitchen laughing. Thomas gave up waiting. "Are you from around here originally?" Thomas smiled at Vance shyly.

Vance glanced indifferently at Thomas. "I'm from the east coast." He concentrated on a bit of fuzz that had somehow attached itself to his plaid shirt. He frowned at the offending intrusion, and despite the large size of his hands, he flicked it off with a delicate snap of his fingers.

This wasn't going well...Thomas tried to make out the delicate trajectory of the offending particle. She was cast on the desert island...she better make the best of it. "Was that a difficult transition?" Her voice sounded wooden even to her.

Vance looked at Thomas blankly as he listened to the laughing in the kitchen. "I'm going to see what's going on." He quickly got up from his chair and sped into the kitchen as if he were escaping from a fire.

Thomas kept nodding benignly to no one in

particular. Finally the nodding stopped; she sagged into the chair…if she only knew what Vance's story was. Perhaps he's lost in a different universe too. If so, there appeared to be no connection, no cosmic worm hole from his universe to hers. She glanced around the room. There, just waiting for her sat *Pride and Prejudice* on the coffee table. She glanced around to see if anybody was watching, then grabbed the book slyly.

"Mrs. Gardiner's caution to Elizabeth was punctually and kindly given on the first favorable opportunity of speaking to her alone; after honestly telling her what she thought, she thus went on: 'You are too sensible a girl Lizzy, to fall in love merely because you are warned against it; and therefore, I am not afraid of speaking openly. Seriously, I would have you be on your guard.'"

The three came back laughing, holding glasses (some 60's patterned glasses of course). Joe handed her a glass. Vance took his seat two feet from Thomas; Joe and Richard sat close together on the other end.

Thomas smiled benevolently at them…okay she must be on her guard…she took a large swallow of the Harvey Wall Banger…grapefruit and gasoline mixed…the warmth on her throat traveled down into her stomach…tentacles of forgetfulness stretching from her stomach to her head…a smaller sip next time. Yes, this was really all right.

Richard began rolling a joint, his fingers delicately and surely twirling the paper around the marijuana.

Thomas had work to do…no time for being stoned… maybe later. She stood up heading to the kitchen.

The three smoked a joint. Thomas didn't need to speak anymore...yes, the pasta...she had her own date with destiny. She stepped into her domain. Little whirls of steam rose from the bean sauce...perfect...she poured the broken pasta into the sauce adding a little water to barely cover it all...broken pasta because this was a left over Monday meal. Things seemed to happen in funny little islands of moments: pouring the wine in the sauce, one moment; pouring the pasta, next moment; chapping parsley while the pasta cooked, next moment: little universes, each insulated by the briefest instant of forgetfulness: those little gaps, memory full of cosmic wormholes connecting universes. The pasta now was bubbling ferociously in the sauce, softening by the second. Convinced that time really wasn't continuous, she turned the flame down, and then in a quite different universe she threw a small handful of the greenest parsley you could imagine into the sauce. Thomas glanced over her shoulder.

Richard stood in the doorway; he looked benign not ironic.

Thomas nodded with the innocence of the moment.

Richard stepped toward Thomas.

Richard stood next to Thomas.

Thomas could feel the warmth of Richard's attention.

She needed to give the pasta a stir.

The pasta was plumping.

Richard watched her. "How are you doing in here?"

Thomas looked at Richard. "I enjoy cooking."

She glanced over at the boiling pot including it in the conversation. "Of course it's just ordinary, but sometimes ordinary is best. It's easier for me to step into it."

Richard moved closer.

She looked at Richard…how handsome he is… Thomas stepped away ever so slightly.

Richard nodded, "I like to get into things…it takes me time too." He didn't step closer.

At that point Thomas decided that she liked Richard, even if he was handsome.

Thomas nodded at the beans and pasta.

Suddenly a big bubble of bean sauce burst exploding into the room.

Thomas looked startle and then giggled. She picked up the wooden spoon and stirred the sauce with gentle apology. She turned back to Richard. "Do you have a family…are you from here?"

Richard settled back as if getting ready to tell a story.

Thomas did like to hear stories…other people's.

"I grew up just a few miles from here. I've always loved the desert."

Thomas nodded while stirring.

"I was lucky with my parents. They always let me know that I could try things out to see what I really wanted to do."

"It sounds like lovely family."

"I enjoy them. How about you?"

Thomas tightened her hold on the wooden spoon; the pasta continued to casually cook. "My father is dead. I didn't like him when I was child, but as a teenager, I learned to love him. He was a democrat, and every year at the precinct caucus he would propose a gay rights plank, and this was long before other people were doing it. I was close to my mom, but I needed to separate a little to see her as a person. The household was kind of fearful, but I knew they loved me."

Joe's voice from the other room called out. "Where's din din?"

Thomas and Richard looked at each other and without premeditation, in a universe of a moment, they hugged. Thomas felt Richard's hand rest on her butt. The hand felt comforting…one separate moment within a boundary, simple.

Then the next moment she smelled the simmering sauce and noticed a bit of chopped parsley she left like a memento on Richard's shirt. Thomas backed off the universe and brushed the parsley away.

Her pasta called to her; she nodded at Richard. "I'll finish up here. Why don't you go join them?" Thomas picked up the lovely blue enamel bowl…a cool color for hot food…she smiled at the contrast.

In this universe she carefully tilted the pan full of luscious steaming pasta y fagiole into the bowl; at first the pasta stubbornly clung to the pan, then slowly it started shifting seduced by time/space. Tentatively at first the pasta began slithering over the edge of the pan, then confidence gathering, the whole mass of the pasta softly flopped down into the bowl making a gentle glopping sound as it reached the bottom of bowl.

On the seventh day she studied her creation…just a

little raw olive oil on the surface, a little more chopped parsley, and finally a generous sprinkling of freshly grated Parmesan on the surface...she rested, satisfied.

Smiling she called out to her guests, "Come on in and sit down." Her voice was rich and full. She placed the bowl in the middle of the table in the dining room taking its place next to the salad and the French bread. Her three companions followed the smell.

Joe poured wine; they sat down around the mirrored table upon which rested bowls for salad and pasta.

Richard brushed his hand over the shiny surface of the table. He looked at Joe. "Do you remember when we found this? It was a mess. "

Joe looked pleased with himself. "Genuine vintage 1960's."

Vance was admiring the plates. To no one in particular he said, "We collect everything from the sixties."

There was a little frozen pause. Thomas filled it in. "Oh how interesting."

Richard captured Joe's attention. "I never thought you'd actually use it."

Joe looked down in exaggerated shame. "I'm just a drunken old queen."

Richard rushed to comfort him. "We sold quite a few things at the shop last week."

Joe was inconsolable. "They were all yours."

"That avocado green lamp of yours was sold."

Joe brightened, "Really?"

Vance stared out the darkening window, his voice

had a tone of forced animation. "We're always on the lookout for anything from that era. We're crazy about it."

Richard chimed it. "And we sold that black and pink ash tray of yours."

Joe smiled with surprise. "Oh really?"

Thomas looked at Vance. "That sounds fun." She motioned to the bowls of food at the center of the table. "Let's eat."

Vance began mechanically shoveling salad into his bowel. "When we were in Phoenix I spotted this terrific end table."

Richard grabbed the pasta bowel glancing over at Joe. "Do you remember that store?"

Joe shook his head. "Much too expensive. But that pole lamp…that was a deal."

Thomas sat there. Vance passed her the salad from one direction and Joe passed her the pasta from the other. Thomas looked with alarm at both suitors and then began giggling. "The devil or the deep blue sea…" She took one bowl in one hand and another bowl in the other hand and set them both down on the table.

Vance glanced at Richard and Joe. "We collect melmac.

Joe looked over at Thomas with just an edge of sarcasm. "They have a whole room of it."

Thomas carefully spooned some pasta onto her plate, then in a feat of dexterity forked some of the pasta into her mouth…just slightly overdone, but the sauce…how nice. She could smell the aroma of the raw olive oil. "Well it certainly sounds nice to have a hobby."

She took a sip of the red wine...good combination. And the meal went on with the background music of conversation about 60's paraphernalia. Each bite was a moment, universes connected, bite by bite.

Last bite taken, she found herself being shooed out of the house...Joe motioning everyone out; leading the procession. The night, cool, black with little pinpoints of light scattered across it, an overwhelming universe. Richard and Vance, familiar with the protocol settled into the canvas butterfly chairs...at night the chairs seemed more like moths, at home in the darkness. Thomas followed suite, positioning herself on the remaining moth whose wing was slightly torn.

Joe, the master of ceremonies ducked into the darkness. He returned with a pile of twigs and branches in his arms. Very solemnly he knelt with the burden in has arms in front of a small Mexican chimney fireplace.

Thomas watched silently, her whole self, expanding beyond space and time...so many years ago, time like a map in front of her...Thomas and Joe had just gotten together...they went camping...something that Thomas didn't like, but he was so in love, he would do anything to be near Joe...it was a chillier than usual that summer night in Minnesota. Thomas sat in front of the dark tent in a darker forest, motionless, not complaining but starting to shiver...he could feel Joe watching her from the darkness, not judging, just concerned. Joe scrambled off into the dark woods...Thomas could hear Joe's hurried movements. His shadowy form came back with an armful of twigs and branches and knelt down in front of the cold fire grate building a delicate edifice there. Thomas watched…Joe lit a match illuminating his hand and face…his face tight with urgency…the fragile edifice of wood burst into flame lighting up the campsite. Joe's face turned toward Thomas, the face full of caring and satisfaction…

Richard's voice announced, "These are vintage 1960 butterfly chairs, very pricey now."

Thomas looked away from that universe and returned to this moment. "They're very nice."

Joe lit the fire. It flashed into flame burnishing the faces of the four with light.

Thomas settled back into the shadowy arms of the butterfly chair.

Joe stood watching the fire, attention far away, perhaps staring at the map of time.

Vance settled back into the shadow of his chair. He was a dark faceless form now. "I worked on the birdhouses today." His voice was softer in the shadows.

Richard's voice had softened too. "They were really in bad shape."

Thomas nodded sagely from her shadow. "Oh."

"First I took them all down and fixed them…there are 7 of them."

Joe's voice came from his shadow. "That's quite a job."

Vance's voice picked up animation the more attention he received. "And then I wanted to find just the right colors. They need to fit in with the color scheme of the house."

Three heads nodded from their shadows.

Vance's voice burst with excitement. "Turquoise and black! But I alternated, one with a turquoise roof and black walls, and then I switched it for the next one.

Thomas felt included. "That sounds lovely."

For the first time in the evening Vance turned toward Thomas, focusing. "What do you like to do?" Vance sounded like a young boy.

Thomas bent over toward Vance. "Actually, lots of things. I like to garden and read...oh and I love movies and writing, and even people sometimes."

Vance's shadow bent over toward Thomas. "Do you want to go to a movie tomorrow night?"

The night exploded into stories...fireworks in the silent night sky...Thomas studied the masculine shadow leaning forward out of the butterfly chair. The glow of the fire shone like stars in Vance's eyes. Thomas leaned forward and in a breathless voice said, "Yes." A story sparkled in her mind...Vance's thick shoulders and strong hands...his tight voice and disdain hiding depths of...Darcy...he seemed unpromising at first. Thomas edged slightly back into the shadow...remember Mrs. Gardiner's caution and also The Wavy Brown Haired Woman's words.

"Better watch out." Joe peered at Thomas.

Thomas sat in the shadow, reading Joe's mind...all you need is a good fuck. Thomas' body moved back into the shadow...so many men, so many stories...she sat there immobile, scenes of failed romance playing... not memories exactly, but fluttering ghosts of loves past, flying around her like moths…she'd done so many foolish romantic empty things…chapters in a poorly written book…what's a girl to do…falling in love again…Marlene Dietrich…a middle aged drooping she-man dressed in black tights sitting on a bar stool trying to look alluring…a girl…how does a girl grow up? Thomas bent forward again glancing shyly at Vance's shadow.

Vance's shadow whispered, "I saw that the *Aviator* is on at that theater on Broadway."

Silence, except for the hum of night.

Thomas' shadow whispered back, "I'd like to go too."

"Are you sure you want too?" Joe teased, or was he warning?

Thomas turned so that she faced Vance directly. "I'd like to spend some time and get to know you."

Joe laughed nervously. "I'm going to go in and cleanup."

Richard discretely followed.

Vance's shadow moved back into the dark butterfly wings.

Thomas tried to pull Vance's attention back. "Do you like to paint?

The flame and perhaps Vance's ardor seemed to be sputtering out. He stared at the house. "I just paint things around the house." His voice flattened, the stories fading into the night.

Thomas took a deep determined breath. "Well that sounds like a good thing to do. What's your house like?"

Vance glanced in Thomas direction. "Oh it's just a house."

The last embers in the fireplace were winking out. Thomas folded her arms around her body; the night felt cool and damp...is this how a girl grows up? It seems so alone...she glanced at the bulky shadow in the chair opposite him.

No movement.

Thomas' arms held her torso in a tight embrace...left holding the bag...talking in a vacuum. In the darkness Thomas shuttered...she's just being a stupid girl, stupid, stupid, girl...ridiculous old man acting like a stupid girl.

Falling into a rabbit hole...she felt a night breeze rush past her...falling...free fall...free...her body relaxing into the chair...privacy, her own private worm hole...so what if she acts like a girl? That's how girls grow up; they take chances. She bent forward on the butterfly wings, like a pilot looking into the distance... she can do what makes sense to her. "Does Wednesday works for you?"

A long silence settled into the dark night. Vance's strained voice issued from the bulky shadow in the butterfly chair "I'll see if I can get off work early on Wednesday." His voice tightened to a high-pitched hum that disappeared into the darkness. Vance's shadowy form stood up, separating from the dark butterfly. He glanced over at the bright lights of the house. "Maybe they need some help;" his voice directed to no one in particular; his shadow fled.

The stars spun around Thomas...growing up is

so alone…if she could have had her dream come true instead of sitting out here with stars circling her head, she would have taken it. The falling into the night sky, was it a consolation prize or something else? She shivered in the cool night air, a tiny form falling into nothingness, to the sound of retreating footsteps.

A door opened and then closed in the distance.

Letting go into darkness, falling…not so bad really…alone at night…falling through a story into who knows what…just relax into it…yes; she could feel the canvas sail beneath her. Her head pressed against the canvas, tipping backwards and down over the edge of the sail, her eyes staring upward in that vast emptiness calling her. She studied the dark sky…not a flat sky of a painting…somebody's idea of a boundary, but something deep with its own force of gravity pulling people beyond the happiest or saddest story. She felt the warm canvas beneath her trembling…her body pressed against those wings as they made a first flicker and then began a long slow powerful flapping, carrying Thomas up into that distance deeper than the stars. Her body rose on the powerful wings…she could see the lights of Tucson beneath her…still further up she flew…a whole continent resting between dark oceans… somewhere down there Danny's ready to go to bed… higher still, further…a black globe spinning against the sun…the source of all her flickering stories…the sun then retreating and becoming a distant star and finally winking out…the sound of the back door opening, it was Joe.

His voice was soft. "Are you all right?"
Thomas nodded slowly.
Joe watched him with silent tenderness.
Thomas felt it. "Sure…everything's fine."
"They're getting ready to leave."
"I'll say goodbye."
Thomas stood up in the darkness.
They both walked inside the house.

Chapter 14

She woke up to a gray sky, her head a block of wet clay, even the birds were mute…Harvey Wallbangers… third morning…Tuesday…Vance's football player body…the invitation and then reluctance. Thomas studied the faces of the pathetic children staring out at her from their picture frames. Why did she find them so annoying? She shifted in the cocoon of her bed…they stare out, orphans stuck in the frames of their stories… it's easier to have people feel sorry for you, easier than sticking a hand out side of the frame. She pulled the covers up around her head leaving one eye and a nose sticking out of her sanctuary…sometimes it doesn't feel worth it to be exposed to the cool morning air. She closed her eyes and settled into the uneasy comfort on this her third day in Tucson.

Her stomach did a somersault…smell of coffee and the taste of French toast seeped into her imagination…

Ralph's coming tonight, maybe Vance tomorrow...men, it's raining men...she opened her eyes barely glancing at the pitiful children...she had things to do. Taking a deep determined breath she stood up on the cool cement floor, did her morning stretches, and got ready for a new day.

Locking up the quiet house, Joe sleeping in it like a memory; Thomas set out for the restaurant...no golden ramparts this morning. The sharp dark mountains jabbed into the chilly gray sky...thank goodness for French toasts...besides she really didn't know if she liked men as friends...she always felt like an orphan girl hungry for attention and willing to do anything or be anything to get HIM to care. Her feet found their own way to the restaurant...it used to be the end of the world when men didn't notice her...thank goodness for coffee in the morning. She glanced up as the shiny chrome restaurant came into view...when was the last time she fell in love so deeply that it seemed darkly final... with Joe, yes Joe...it felt like the end of everything that was good in life...at first Thomas hoped that that excitement would come again, some new knight who would take her into the sunset...would she really even want to do that again...being held hostage...holding herself hostage...she may be seeing Vance tomorrow night...what's that all about? Thomas pushed the door of the restaurant open and once again was engulfed in the aroma of pleasure...those forays into romance, so fleeting like movies ...then one morning...that's when

Thomas started to garden…a cup of coffee was pushed in front of her across the counter.

She looked up. The Waitress asked her if she wanted the usual. Thomas smiled and nodded…Joe, that was the last time she fell into that deep bottomless hole… now there were ditches with men's names on. "Yes, I want that today…thanks"

The Waitress nodded, smiled and disappeared.

Thomas reached into her pocket…empty…no *Pride and Prejudice* this morning. She smiled, her hand reaching for one of the cream containers…so much to do today. Cavalierly she opened the container and flipped it over, spilling the white contents into the cup of coffee…magic… a stream of white entered the coffee and became a slowly swirling cloud…those ditches not very deep now …still scary to trip into…stumbling while the world watched…being a woman seemed to help, having some sort of path that wasn't just leading to a man she couldn't have, or a man she didn't want… more open…preposterous but personal…Danny thinks Thomas just wants to avoid sex…maybe…with guys it seems to always be about sex. She stirred the cloud into the coffee; it turned a deep creamy uniform brown… at first it seemed just a crazy idea that she thought she was a woman inside…a weird cloud in the coffee of her life, but when she started letting people in on her secret, her life started changing in a strange way. The waitress softly slid her breakfast along the counter and into her reverie. Thomas glanced up at her.

A faint looked of recognition flickered across The Waitress's face as she turned away.

Thomas bent her head over the plate smelling it and picked up her fork...a good day to die...being a man never really made sense like French toast do or even the feel of a stubbornly gray cold morning...she could fake it of course, but she always ended up being a poor imitation of a boy who felt like a girl...no growing up there, and grownups can do some things that children can't, like driving a car or making friends, or getting married, or actually living a life...Thomas could only pretend until she started becoming a woman...at least that's how it seemed. She soaked up the last of the syrup with her French toast. This time she left a little wedge of sausage on the plate just for the fun of it. She had choices, after all.

The Waitress had such lovely timing; she walked over to Thomas and said, "Have a nice morning."

Why, this morning was full of imagination...little things and moments she wasn't afraid of. "You too, you're a wonderful person."

"Thanks honey." And she was off and so was Thomas.

This morning seemed so full of possibilities, even with a gray chilly sky...art galleries, that's what she wanted to see today...buses are so wonderful...Ralph was coming tonight...funny to meet someone who was supposed to be like yourself...she had always been with men who were very different than herself. She crossed Broadway to the bus stop...who knows she might even consider buying a painting…that's probably going too far…buying something for herself to put in the place she was living in…home, really just temporary apartments or other people's houses…home…what is a home? She had started gardening when she moved in with Danny… that's something, anyway. She sat down on the bus bench on that chilly morning, dark mountains listening to her over her shoulders. Children don't have their own houses; they rely on adults to make homes…Thomas frowned at the traffic streaming in front of her…she could hear the deep rumbling of an approaching bus… making a home beautiful had been something for other people…happenstance was for Thomas…she stepped onto the bus.

The bus roared beneath her as it headed into the city.

Stepping off the bus, people in business suites rushed around her like frantic ants…she had never really bought anything to make her life beautiful… there was a series of used sofas and chairs that friends had bequeathed to him…useful shabby things to fill her temporary abodes…then of course when she moved in with a man; it was someone else's house, and she was a lodger. Thomas meandered past shop windows in which beautiful things were displayed behind glass…so close but so absolutely unapproachable…she pressed her hand against the cool glass separating her from beauty…a land of dreams under glass.

She stopped in front one broad window…strange black and white pictures: sad eyed Madonna's with scorpion bodies, babies flying in the air with bat wings, mysterious Sacred Hearts throbbing with pain and ecstasy...a gallery. She stepped through the door and into that world of sacred metamorphosis. Those prints were hanging on all the walls...$1000...yikes! She studied each print...the anguish and wonder mixed together. A slim dramatic looking woman...you could just tell that she loved art...stepped up to Thomas. "Can I help you with something?"

For a moment Thomas felt like an impostor, and the woman sounded so focused, so earnest, so hopeful. For a moment Thomas felt like a child pretending to be an adult...what would a woman do? "I really like these prints. Something about them is mysterious, but still I kind of understand them."

The Dramatic Looking Woman nodded reassuringly. "He's an extraordinary artist combining a technical mastery of woodcut printing with an almost childlike sense of awe." Her voice sounded rehearsed as she nodded knowingly.

Thomas became flustered. "I really don't have the kind of money to buy something like this."

The Dramatic Woman moved closer to him. "They're a real bargain. He's one of the top figures in the Tucson art world." She looked Thomas in the eye, "A good investment."

Her irises were sky blue, but in the middle of them two holes as bottomless as night stared at Thomas; she could see her own image reflected on the shiny surface of The Dramatic Woman's eyeballs. Thomas raised the gaze of her eye above those sky blue curtains that veiled night; she raised her gaze to the middle of The Dramatic Woman's forehead. "Thank you very much. They certainly are beautiful…I don't want to spend that amount of money now."

Thomas watched the crease between The Dramatic Woman's eye deepen…the sausage was really wonderful this morning, but Thomas didn't want to eat that last bit. She smiled with some confidence at The Dramatic Woman.

Though The Dramatic Woman was looking directly at Thomas her attention now disappeared. She glanced at a man in a business suite who had just entered the gallery. She took her gaze off Thomas and said to no one in particular, "He really does wonderful work."

Thomas looked at a print. "They're beautiful."

Whatever gravity that had drawn her to Thomas had passed; The Dramatic Woman's whole body was being pulled toward a man in a suite who had just entered the store; her feet now obeyed the force of gravity. She left behind a business-like, "Excuse me."

In her wake Thomas said, "You have been very helpful." And she had…it was Danny's house after all…a thousand dollars…she shook her head; it was really too much. She stepped out of the gallery into the rush of people on the sidewalk and placed her body up against the window; once gain she stared in at that forbidden world beyond the glass. Will she ever grow up?

Thomas returned to Joe's place just as he was getting up…padding around the house with a hangdog look

on his face…reassuring…he did that thirty years ago…
timeless.

Joe disappeared into the kitchen. Thomas heard
the refrigerator open and the sound of a beer bottle cap
being popped off.

Thomas aimed his voice at the kitchen. "Do you
think Vance actually wants to go to a movie with me?"

No answer from the kitchen. Thomas stared off
into the distance, frowning. First her feet twitched,
then her shoulders shifted, and finally as if propelled
by some inner urgency she jumped up and walked into
the kitchen.

Joe was pouring himself a glass of beer. The clouds
must have passed because the sun shone from the
window and through Joe's amber colored glass of beer.

Thomas stood in the kitchen, her hands on his
hips. "Do you think Vance actually wants to go to the
movie with me?"

Silence, as Joe stared at the topaz in his hand…it
was like a scene in a Vermeer painting, "Man Looking
at Glass of Beer in the Window."

Thomas's body began slackening, her eyes entranced
by the jewel, wondering about the long distance magic
of the sun. Her body tensed again. "Well, what do you
think?"

Joe laughed softly. "He's your boyfriend not mine."

Thomas bridled. "You're the one that's sleeping
with him."

Joe studied Thomas slyly. "You always have to
control everything."

"Forget it."

Joe looked up from his jeweled glass and moaned pathetically. "Just wait and see for once. You always have to makes things so complicated."

"I don't know."

They glanced at each other for a flicker of a moment. Joe smiled. "You need a good fuck."

Thomas smiled back. "You need your head examined."

"How about a beer?"

"Too early in the day."

"I'm going to the gallery today."

"Can I come?"

Joe turned around. "Pigface."

"I'd like to see your show."

Joe nodded slowly. "I want you to."

They headed off a half an hour later in the truck that smelled of pee. Joe drove with a quiet resolve through the outskirts of Tucson, the funky city turning into the land of high priced castles and walled communities. The sun shone more brightly as they drove higher up into the mountains. Thomas sighed as she gazed out the window. " How's it going with Tim? When did you make it final?"

"He was really mad at me. When he was cleaning out the computer after I left the house, he found some pictures of Richard and I." He looked over at Thomas with exaggerated remorse…a real feeling casting a larger than life shadow.

"Yikes!" Thomas toned down his surprise. "That

must have been really hard for Tim to see you two when he was in love with you."

"That's not all. Richard used to work for us. I told Tim that we didn't start messing around until I was out of the company. I'm a whore."

"Tim thinks I'm ruining my life."

"Your life?"

"Selfish Joe."

"I don't mean it that way. Like…" Thomas struggled for words. "It's like you're not selfish enough. You live the way you think we want you to live. You can live anyway you want and figure things out from there."

"All I do is hurt people, Tim and you and everyone else." Joe's body seemed to shrink against the car seat.

Thomas stared out the window as if looking for a clue to a mystery. "I don't know about everyone else, but I don't feel that way. Sure, we knocked each other up a bit, but this is my life I'm living and everything that happens to me is something…" Her words got stuck in her throat.

"You're just trying to be nice."

Thomas coughed softly. "I'm not nice. You know that." She stared fiercely at Joe. "Everybody's life…it's just that we're all doing the best we can and maybe we can learn something as we go."

"Pigface needs a fuck."

"Goofball." Thomas looked back out the window.

Joe nodded slowly. "I have to get busy, I have a show to do. My agent keeps pushing me; she needs to or bum Joe won't get anything done."

They were in the mountains now, the housing communities dwarfed by the jagged mountains. With all the rain recently, the reddish brown mountains were brushed with wisps of green.

Joe looked straight ahead. "Good bloom this year."

They drove over a ridge; the mountain came right down to the road. Then they were up and over to the other side; below was a bowl of a valley with peaks all around it.

"It's not a very big gallery."

They approached what looked like an expensive shopping mall; the truck pulled into a parking lot and stopped in front of a store. The shopping mall and the whole bowl of a valley seemed strangely empty except for a few cars driving by…some distant god's creation of a world that he hadn't peopled yet. Thomas stepped out of the car. "It's cooler up here."

The wind gusted in dry cold jabs. They walked solemnly to the glossy looking gallery. Joe tugged at the door. It didn't budge. "She said she'd be here." He looked at Thomas apologetically.

An expensive ghost town…perhaps there had been a nuclear war down in the world of people below… every human being had died of radiation poisoning… waltzing Matilda, waltzing Matilda… leaving a chic expensive empty shell…for some unexplained reason Thomas and Joe were the only survivors on the beach of human existence. "Can I look through the windows?"

They both pushed their faces up against the window, cold dead glass against their noses, hands to their faces like visors to block out light, eyes searching the artifacts of a defunct world behind the glass. Moisture from their breath created little clouds on the glass, the only sign of life.

Thomas studied the artifacts of a dead world. "There's some really beautiful things in there." It was indeed the kind of gallery that smelled like money, small, but nothing could be touched for less than thousands of dollars...when humans lived on earth.

Joe stepped back from the glass. "Some of it's pretty hokey. Do you see over there?"

Thomas pressed her face closer, her forehead and chin touching the cold glass.

"Those are mine." Joe sounded proud, no false remorse.

Thomas's eyes explored the paintings along the side wall...paintings for the end of the world...the shapes moving back and forth across the time...a memory of life now forever gone. "Those are wonderful."

"Bum Joe"

Thomas stepped back leaving the cloud on the glass, emotional archaeology. She studied their two reflections in the glass...insubstantial, not even alive...a trick of light and darkness and glass. Even the breath-cloud was disappearing. Their images simultaneously turned around leaving the ghost gallery at peace.

By the time they were headed down the mountains everything was turning dark and lights all over the town below were sparking on; dark windowed companion cars hummed along the highway, still no people in sight. Thomas looked over at Joe. "What time is Ralph coming over tonight?"

Joe seemed matter of fact. "He said he'd come at about 7:00. Where do you want to eat?"

They were back in the ordinary world of the living. "I don't care, but let's go Dutch."

"Big spender." He rolled his eyes.

"How old is Ralph?"

"About forty."

"Yikes he's young!" The car hummed along joining those other dark windowed cars heading to their destinations.

Even though it wasn't a date, Thomas showered and put on a fancy shirt, a deep purple blue with a repeating pattern of flimsy hope and despair.

For this evening Joe had placed another bowl of potato chips on the coffee table. "Do you want a drink?"

Thomas thought about it. "Maybe I'll wait." She sat down; there beside her waited *Pride and Prejudice.* 'More than once did Elizabeth in her rambling within the park unexpectedly meet Mr. Darcy. She felt all the perverseness of the mischance that should bring him where no one else was brought." She was startled by the sound of the doorbell…here we go again…she closed the book…face tightening into what she hoped looked like calm. Joe opened the door. Thomas sat there for a moment taking a deep breath…break a leg.

Another man in a baseball cap…a narrow face, a sparse goatee, delicate hands waved in the air as he embraced Joe…his face under the casual pretense of a baseball cap was tight around the eyes. Joe and Ralph hugged; Joe broke away from the embrace a little too forcefully. "Ralph, this is my friend Thomas."

Ralph examined Thomas for an instant and then extended his hand tentatively.

Thomas grasped it. It felt cool and soft...no visions of masculinity...no savior in a ghost town here. "I've heard so many nice things about you. I just decided that I'd like to meet you. Joe said that we had some things in common."

Ralph's hands waved in the air delicately. "Don't believe a word he says." He had a soft voice, not campy, but with just the hint of a southern drawl.

Thomas forgave him for the baseball cap.

Ralph's hands stopped waving, but his eyes remained tight with some kind of hidden effort.

Thomas understood hidden effort, those parts of the secret self too hard to share.

"How about some wine?" Joe was at his most genial.

Ralph's face relaxed as he gazed at Joe...that special look of being in the presence of the beloved...Thomas knew it so well.

She watched and remembered...years ago when Joe and Thomas were together he learned to recognize that look, in fact his whole attention was focused on men who loved Joe. Thomas hated them and knew it was just a matter of time until Joe had an affair with them, but he was too desperate to be angry at Joe.

She moved her attention away from Joe and Ralph... it was so much easier now...besides she didn't have a date with Ralph and she certainly was no longer with Joe…how nice…let them sort out their own business. She sat down on the sofa, content.

Joe left the room to get drinks, leaving Thomas and Ralph. Ralph sat down two feet from Thomas. "When did you get in?"

"A few days ago. You know I've been here before."

Ralph gazed warily at Thomas. Was Ralph trying to see if Thomas was competition? "It's fun to see Joe. Once we were partners, but that was decades ago." She looked Ralph right in the eyes. "It's such a relief to know that it's just a friendship. Romance was such a misunderstanding for both of us."

Ralph's face relaxed.

Thomas nodded to emphasize the death of romance and started giggling in relief.

Ralph looked a little confused.

"I was just thinking how dramatic things were once and now it all seems so unimportant."

Ralph looked reassured now.

"So Joe said that you are the father of a boy and you're raising him with two mothers…sounds very creative."

Ralph studied Thomas for a moment to see if she was making fun of him.

Thomas's face was filled with benign interest.

The tightness around Ralph's eyes began to soften. He bent forward in intimacy. "It didn't seem like it at the time, but things just kind of fell into place."

"That's sounds lovely."

"I suppose this sounds like every parent, but then the hard work starts. I wouldn't change it, but it's pretty demanding. And then I really have to work with my relationship with the two mothers."

"Threesome's can be hard. I was once in a business relationship with two other people." She shook his head solemnly. "Three people..."

Joe came back into the room carrying three glasses and a bottle of wine. "How about a little smoke?"

Ralph looked at Joe again with that special look of love; then he glanced at Thomas as if for permission.

Thomas smiled and nodded.

Joe poured the wine. "What are you two guys talking about?"

Thomas looked protectively at Ralph. "None of your business, dear." She and Ralph exchanged a knowing look.

Joe began rolling a joint. "I'm horrible at this." He offered the bag and papers to Ralph.

Ralph shook his head emphatically. "Maybe Thomas..."

Joe rolled his eyes.

Thomas frowned archly at Joe. "Sure, sounds like fun."

"I remember how you used to roll joints." Joe shook his head condescendingly.

Thomas reached over to take bag and papers. "Live and learn."

Joe was silenced.

Thomas fingered the paper and marijuana...only

boys can whistle, only men roll joints tightly…funny how she had always passed this task on to the man. The joint looking like a white flower now going backwards into time to become a bud…silly to make the males of her life be men so that on the sly she could be a girl… women can do things by themselves. And there it was a fairly tight elongated white bud. She passed it to Joe.

Joe lit the joint and took a puff and passed it on to Ralph.

Ralph hand trembled slightly as his fingers delicately wrapped around the joint. He took a long drawn out drag, held his breath and then slowly released the cloud of smoke, his face opening like a flower as he gazed at Joe…the color of hope and yearning.

Joe backed away ever so slightly.

The flower faded.

Thomas watched inconspicuously…she and Ralph did have much in common. Thomas felt a little twinge of sadness for all those unanswered prayers placed at the altar of The Man. She squeezed the white bud gently between his fingers…no, she wasn't going to smoke tonight and smiled at Ralph as she passed the joint. "I was telling Joe that I've started to see myself as a woman."

Joe laughed. "Oh no! I thought you said that you weren't going to embarrass me."

Thomas looked sheepish for just an instant and then started laughing as if that indeed was a good joke. "I'm a hopeless cause." He laughed. "And fuck you too."

Joe and Thomas laughed hysterically.

Ralph watched them, confused again.

Thomas turned to Ralph. "You see inside I feel I am a woman...it just feels that way. It kind of explains so much, so many misunderstandings. Being gay was the closest category I could find. I am a physical male attracted to men. But inside the real me...that's female." She looked over at Joe. "Here I was trying to make Joe into my husband when he didn't want a wife. And I spent all my time trying to be a good girl instead of growing up into a woman." She laughed to herself and suddenly turned to Ralph. "Do you perceive yourself as male or female...the inside part?"

Ralph looked startled.

Thomas tilted her head slightly as she watched Ralph's face.

Even behind his smoky veil, confusion, shame, irritation, and anger shifted across Ralph's face. He touched his baseball hat for reassurance; his eyes tightened again.

Thomas gave Ralph an apologetic look. "I ask the craziest questions; just ask Joe. You can tell me to shut up." She tried to look like an embarrassed old lady... not a threat, just foolish.

Ralph blurted out, his voice deepening, "I see myself as a man." He took a deep breath. He frowned as if he weren't quite sure where that answer came from.

Thomas nodded softly. "It's not really important for anyone else. Knowing I am growing up to be a woman helps me sort of contain myself, not like a wall, but like knowing in what direction I'm going in." She shook her head softly. "So much misunderstanding and hurt when people don't know where they're going."

The joint sat on the ashtray...the little snake of smoke hovering above it getting thinner and thinner. Finally the joint gave a little gasp and sat there dead as a snake skin.

Chapter 15

The constant ticking sound that she had grown used too suddenly stopped…for an instant Thomas woke to booming silence…another morning. She woke up at the very instant that time disappeared. The blue window, the pouting children, her life with Danny or Joe, having a job, even the body lying in bed…all still there, all there still, disappearing wisps of something. Only the waves of breath mattered now, now, and it was the world breathing, not herself…waves of breath passing through. From somewhere in the ocean a siren blared, time began ticking again. Thomas felt her life begin moving forward again, in the sequence of time, past present, future: the old conveyor belt…the fourth morning of her trip. She pushed the covers off and sat on the edge of the bed. In her mind's eye she could see Danny in his black suite, sitting at his desk; she must give Danny a call.

From 1500 miles away, a voice came through the receiver. "Good morning, Danny Rourke here."

Thomas smiled, "Good morning dear."

"Hi honey, how are you doing?"

"Just fine, I had supper with Joe and a friend last night. How are you doing?"

"Work's been hectic. Bob and I went out last night to watch the boys at Wilde Roast. Same old same old."

"Oh."

"I miss you."

"Thanks honey."

"Your bother Dave called. He wants to set up a breakfast date. I never knew a family that got together so much."

"Did you remind him that I'm away?"

"Yes... I wrote a new annual appeal letter. Bill and Joan were really impressed. One more month and my probation is over. They just don't know a thing about fund raising. They sign off on my ideas, but I know they're not going to do anything about them. I tell you, they don't know a thing."

"Maybe you can teach them."

"If they ever listen to me..."

"I'm just headed out for the day. You take care, dear."

"I love you."

"I love you too."

Pictures of Vance flashed through Thomas's mind, propelling him into the future...thick shoulders, strong hands, the funny captured way he spoke...this evening... oh don't be silly. She put the phone down.

Before Vance fled two nights ago, he left a lingering "I'll see if I can get off work early on Wednesday." Thomas shook her head. Is that a promise or an excuse? Once again she dangled in suspense, twisting and turning, hanging from the words of a man, promises or rejections pulling her through time.

The conveyor belt of her day pushed her forward... breakfast, eggs, sausage, and French toast..."Have a nice day honey," all were markers of her movement toward the phone call from Vance. Her steps began moving by themselves, each step ticking through time, measuring anticipation.

The pace of her feet slowed down in the walled tower of anticipation. Her life had always been so full of activities that would hasten the forward movement to Never-land...watching movies or reading or masturbating or even being with people. Her placid face tightened, but you see up in that tower you still grow old...old...less and less chances of being rescued... princes threadbare or non-existent. Finally she's just old and she's never really learned anything, never even felt anything except wanting time to go by faster, waiting for something or someone to happen.

She stepped outside and only saw her own private picture postcard of Tucson, two dimensional, flat, a picture of mountains towering over the houses. She was not really in the picture, just looking at it from the outside. How does that happen? She remembered waking this morning, waking to the world breathing through her, and now, now this flatness, living on promises or excuses. Like some curse the world had become flattened; everything she touched turned inanimate. Her face softened in grief as her feet kept plodding slowly along the pavement to the sound of the regular beat of the clock. Why was she doing this again? No answer; Postcards are silent.

A cool morning breeze suddenly whispered through her. A flicker of a smile passed through her awareness and across her face…yes, she flew through space two evenings ago…flying. What about talking with Joe in the van and being fierce, and watching Ralph being in love with Joe and just feeling relief. It wasn't just waiting…it's getting dirty…girls can learn when they get dirty…when they try things out. Getting dirty, what does that mean? Of course Joe thinks it has something to do with being fucked. She supposed that is a kind of getting dirty for some girls, but Thomas had plenty of that in New York years ago.

She pondered these questions as she ate her usual breakfast, The Waitress, her only witness. Maybe getting dirty is just surviving, living through experiences. Does it really matter after all if those experiences are misfortune or success? The thing is to live with the happening, living as time disappears.

Back at Joe's now, pacing to the beat of time and men. She's back in the tower and life is walled away somewhere…live through this, even this flatness of anticipation. Thomas could see the hands of the clock in the kitchen moving slowly, oh so slowly toward 3:00. That's when Vance said he would be out of work, and he'll call. It was only 11:00. Four more hours…demurely she sat on the sofa, and there waiting for her sat *Pride and Prejudice,* time still ticking as she opened the book. "Elizabeth awoke the next morning to the same thoughts and meditations which had at length closed her eyes. She could not yet recover from the surprise of what had happened; it was impossible to think of anything else." Thomas looked up from her book.

Joe staggered to the bathroom…shuffling sounds… urine splashing in the bowl…water running in the sink. He staggered out, dragging himself through the living room on the way to the kitchen. He glanced at Thomas. "I'm a bum."

Thomas glances up at him anxiously. "I don't have time for that."

"What's got into you?"

Thomas looked down in confusion. "It's this Vance thing."

"Oh no, Pigface is in trouble. Give him more antidepressants.

"You're a lot of help."

"How about a beer?" Joe shuffled into the kitchen.

Thomas got up following him. "I'll try a beer."

They stood opposite each other in the kitchen, each holding a beer, just standing there in their own worlds.

Joe took a sip.

Thomas watched him. "You know the thing about the movie with Vance?"

"I told you to be careful."

"Ya, ya, ya."

Relenting, Joe smiled. "Vance is strange."

Thomas looked at the clock, 12:00 noon. It's not what you're thinking…it's not a date."

Joe smiled skeptically. "Oh ya?"

"It can't be. I'm married and I don't do things like that."

"Little Miss Perfect. At least be honest with yourself."

"Oh shit…I'm like that?"

"I'm a bum."

"Would you stop that?"

Joe stared at Thomas. "Would you stop that?"

Thomas took a big swallow of beer. "Oh Christ!"

Joe looked very serious. "I don't know if he'll call. He's really confused."

"You must hate me."

"Be a bad girl for once."

"You know I was never very good at that."

"You're telling me!"

"Ya, I know…so what do you think I ought to do about Vance?"

Joe studied Thomas with soft eyes. "If he doesn't call by 4:00, call him."

"That's a plan." Thomas looked relieved.

Joe took a long drink.

"Things are so fucking weird."

Pigface." Joe wondered into his studio.

Thomas stood by the sink, a beer in his hand, staring out the window on a bright dry desert garden in the middle of winter. It's okay really. Joe sees her, and maybe even Danny sees her, but can she live with the mess of wanting things that don't make sense? She stared at the clock willing the hands to move faster. The clock stubbornly resisted, in fact it may have actually decided to move more slowly.

3:00 PM, no call. It's 4:00 PM now; no call from Vance...years of lonely exile in a tower...not so bad really, just kind of weird.

She picked up a phone, her fingers slowly reverently press the buttons...an in between state, a super-positioning of possibilities waiting to be born. "Hi Vance, it's Thomas, Joe's friend."

There was a pause on the other end; then a tight mechanical voice crossed the air waves. "I had such a busy day at work. I just spaced out on the sofa listening to tunes with a glass of beer and a bowl of chips."

Thomas was wondering if this was some sort of code she should be interpreting...fuck codes. "I was wondering if you would like to go to a movie tonight?"

"Hey, how's your vacation going?"

For a moment Thomas was baffled. Are they speaking the same language? This was the moment she had been most afraid of...a man casually not seeing her and not even remembering.

"I had a busy day at work today; I'm gonna take it easy. I'm not that crazy about movies."

There it is, falling inward; her eyes looked out from the land of the dead...Egyptian Eye. How strangely quiet, the booming of time, suddenly silent. She could hear the murmur of her own breath, feel the heat of the plastic receiver against her ear.

"Maybe we'll see you before you leave." Vance's voice was very casual.

"That might be nice." Thomas slowly put down the receiver. She heard a pebble splash as it reached the bottom of the well; she was the pebble. Brushing herself off, she was alive, strangely peaceful. Maybe this was how Lazarus felt waking up wrapped in bandages suddenly summoned back to life…nothing solemn about it…just breathing…maybe even feeling a sly sense of irony.

She walked into Joe's studio. "No fool like an old fool."

Joe sitting at his computer glanced up.

They looked at each other.

Thomas finally rolled her eyes and smiled. "It's not as bad as it used to feel, but I still get carried away for a while."

Joe groaned merrily, "You need a good fuck."

Thomas narrowed her eyes and smiled. "You're still out of your mind."

"You need to get in trouble."

"I got in trouble when I met you."

"I'm a bum."

"I have to get in trouble my own way."

"Then do it."

"I am. That's what I have been doing."

"You call that trouble?"

"Yup." Thomas shrugged and left the room. She sat next to her book. "She grew absolutely ashamed of herself. Of neither Darcy nor Wickham could she think without feeling that she had been blind, partial, prejudiced, absurd."

Thomas whispered, "Absurd, what's wrong with absurd?" She heard the phone ring in Joe's study and slowly closed the book, space and time thinning.

A voice from far away called out. "Richard called."

The world started materializing.

The voice from the study latched on to Thomas. "He invited us to listen to Vance sing karaoke at the bar tonight."

Thomas found herself sitting in Tucson, in late afternoon with a book in her lap, ghosts fluttering about. "You gotta be kidding."

Joe peeked his head into the living room. "You gotta to see it too believe it."

For a moment they balanced on the edge of nowhere, laughing like crazy people.

"I wouldn't miss it for the world."

Chapter 16

T hey walked into the gay bar at 9:00 PM, and it was almost empty except for a handsome young waiter, thin as a willow with a mysterious smile on his face. He nodded towards the two new arrivals nonchalantly and slowly, gracefully transplanting himself next to their table. "Can I get you something?"

Joe frowned at nobody in particular. "A Corona."

The waiter distractedly nodded at Thomas.

She hesitated. "Oh, give me one, too."

Joe watched the waiter ever so gracefully leave the table. "Handsome man."

She nodded, "I suppose so."

Joe and Thomas sat there at a loss for words… decades ago, even when they were at the peek of their romance, they really had little to say to each other. Now sitting opposite each other Thomas drifted off. Years ago she would follow Joe to gay bars, two or three nights a week. It took a couple of years of that for Thomas to decide that she hated to stay up late and one drink was about all she could take...there was a strange sameness to bars, even the men started to look alike. She stopped going, leaving Joe to all the possibilities there.

The Handsome Waiter reappeared at their table with two large glasses of beer. He and Joe talked briefly...Joe must be a regular here. Thomas sat there invisible except for the thrill of damp coolness in her hand as she grasped the glass...she was a ghost again, invisible except when she made a fool of herself...a nuisance. When did she become a nuisance? Exactly at what point in the clock of her life did that transformation take place? She raised the glass to her lips as Joe and the waiter circled each other with words. Foam on her upper lip...cool...then the cold liquid pouring down her mouth...she could feel it right to her stomach. If this is being a ghost, it's under rated, such simple pleasures.

Joe looked troubled as The Handsome Waiter floated away.

In whatever stream of movement in which Joe and the waiter moved, she, Thomas was on a kind of shore of simple pleasure.

They drank their beers in silence.

As the evening flowed on Thomas watched the world float by...so many misunderstandings.

Richard and Vance made their entrance; two handsome men. There was a swirl of attention around them, heads turning, positions on bar stools shifting... the nightly bar show beginning in earnest. As Richard and Vance encountered the rapids of other men's yearning, their bodies seemed to shimmer.

Vance, a star, studied his sheets of music, cutting through the glances of the men at the bar, his obliviousness…a magnet for their fantasies.

Richard, for this magic night was Vance's foil, walked behind in the wake of Vance's glamour, nodding at the attentive faces.

The duo passed through the rapids with ease and approached Joe and Thomas.

Thomas's hand tightened around the glass…the damp coolness in her hand reminding her of life on the shore. She smiled benevolently, nodding to the duo.

They took their seats at the table. Vance, the celebrant of the mystery was clothed in a bowling shirt, the fabric shiny and draping smoothly over his strong torso…the priest becoming god.

Thomas glanced over at the spectacle of Vance, so masculine and distracted. The sacrament of fascination began drawing Thomas into the river. She raised her glass to remind herself of her ghostly perspective…the coolness of the rim of the glass on her lower lip, then the sour cold taste flowing into her mouth…shore.

Richard sat opposite Joe. Richard's head bobbed back and forth between Joe and Vance.

Vance looked up from the sheets of music. He let out a high pitched, nervous giggle. Then his face and his whole body metamorphosed. His voice rang out, deep and confident, "This will do."

Richard's head was drawn toward the priest, Joe, momentarily abandoned.

The Handsome Waiter swirled back to the table. Vance and Richard ordered a drink.

Joe scowled at The Waiter and ordered another drink.

The Waiter smiled condescendingly.

As Thomas glanced over the top of her glass, she sensed that something was amiss between the four attractive men.

Joe got up to go the bathroom.

Richard looked over at Thomas with alarm. "He seems so depressed tonight." He looked over at Vance who gave an absentminded nod.

Thomas glanced in Joe's direction. "He is?"

This was assent enough for Richard. "What can we do to cheer him up?"

"He seems all right...about the same as usual."

Richard was oblivious to the negative. "We were here last week. Joe had a little too much to drink, and the waiter was flirting with me. Joe made a scene."

The glass in Thomas' hand was beginning to warm...funny how things find an equilibrium. She tried to look as kind as possible. "I remember when Joe and I were together. I spent more time being alarmed by Joe's drinking...seems it was the most important thing in my life." He glanced over at Richard.

"But I want to help."

"Ya?" Thomas looked doubtful.

"We need to do something." Dramatic urgency lit Richard's eyes.

Thomas put her glass down directly in front of herself...she could still feel the some coolness on her hand as the moisture evaporated. "It took a while, but I pretty much learned to stay out of his head and get on with things. In some weird way he fed off my attention. And I wasn't doing him or myself a favor"

Richard looked troubled and then straightened Vance's shirt so that it would hang just right.

Joe came back.

An old heavy-set man, another ghost, began fiddling with the sound system on the make-shift stage in the center of the wooden dance floor...funny how ghosts appear and disappear...a form of magic.

Even though Vance didn't look up, he took off his baseball cap, picked up his pile of music and began slowly rising from his chair. All the time an amazing transformation was taking place; his face, usually a handsome mask, began to sparkle with animation; a breathtaking smile flashed at his audience. The handsome bulk of his body sprung to life as he walked to the stage.

All eyes were on him; the music started. His strong hand grasped the microphone, his shirt shimmering under the spot-light, and though the words of the song flashed on the wall above the bar, all eyes were fixed on this Lord of the Night. He looked out over the audience, his gaze too broad and encompassing to focus on any one person...a moment of suspense as he paused, wrapping himself in the fantasies projected by his audience. A smile of triumph flickered across his face...long live the king...his strong male voice, plenty of base, filled the bar with its magnificent if not always tuneful majesty. He reigned for the length of the song as the king and victim of people's needs.

Thomas watched the blessed sacrament by which grace the audience was allowed to experience a dream come true. Thomas shifted uncomfortable on the hard bar chair... middle aged bodies exert their need to move.

"Tie a yellow ribbon round the old oak tree..."

She glanced around the table. Richard watched proudly while Joe finished his second glass of beer and waved the waiter to bring another.

When the music ended Vance looked lost for the briefest of moments, and then everyone clapped shoring up his glamour temporarily. He put the microphone down and walked back to his table. Just as he sat down another handsome man walked up to the stage and for the length of the next song became a star...the king is dead; long live the king.

Chapter 17

She woke the next morning among the gallery of the wounded children who wait for something that they could only imagine. She whispered to the children, "I'm sorry that things are hard for you." They looked out from their pictures, motionless. She studied the pictures carefully in hopes of finding some sign of life and thought she noticed that a wide eyed puppy in the grip of a wider eyed girl might have stirred just slightly. She listened for silence in the house and then whispered gently to the whole room, "I know that you're listening. Don't worry, I know you're alive."

She got up from the warm bed, her right hip ached slightly as she stepped on the cool floor...things to do today; she walked to the bathroom, sat down and peed among the dogs and horses. a hot shower, steam enveloped her like a warm cloud. She stepped out of the cloud, grabbed a towel and slowly with tender care dried each part of her aging body, dressed, said goodbye to the children and walked off towards French toast and sausage and coffee and eggs and a real person wishing her a nice day…so many things to do, Thursday, her fifth and last day in Tucson.

She walked that morning towards The American Café, already the mountains around her were beginning to fade slightly… universe disappearing, evaporating before her eyes…not that she actually believed in time, but there seemed to be geographies of imagination, connected in some strange way, and if you squinted your eyes and disregarded the complexities of experience… well, you really could approximate something called "time." But if you didn't try too hard to focus, time and space tend to disappear…leaving what? Maybe a strange sense of possibility, a kind of superposition that could be anywhere, anytime, even anyone. She focused and her steps took on the approximation of purpose…she wanted to buy something for Joe. How many cities and for how many years had she searched for something, something that Joe would like or even better, be amazed by, even if he wasn't amazed by her.

The Waitress seemed to sense Thomas fading ever so slightly; she held Thomas in her gaze slightly longer than usual as if creating a memory. Then she wished him "a good day." After all her universe was shifting, too.

Thomas headed for the bus stop. She sat down on the bench by Broadway and closed her eyes. Without movement and memory there couldn't be time… a holy trinity, ephemeral but strangely useful to create enchantments. She heard the approaching rumble of a bus; opened her eyes; stood up. The bus stopped right in front of her. The doors folded open with a sweeping sound. The fare box sucked up her dollar. As it disappeared, she said, "Nice day" to the driver who glanced her way and said, "Yup."

Thomas sat down with the other passengers…late morning now…busy, serious people had long since arrived at whatever destinations that enabled them to earn money and survive. The bus now was occupied by ghosts, people on the shore who on weekday mornings didn't have destinations to make them feel safe. As inconspicuously as she was able, she studied each passenger…maybe ghosts are just people traveling between worlds, people not completely anchored to a situation…maybe that's why they seem to kind of flicker in and out to observers who are anchored, maybe even trapped in their universes. She smiled…she was in such good company.

She got off at the end of the line and started walking towards 4th St, down the underground walkway and up again to a different world. In the 60's and 70's Thomas was a youthful vision for someone else's eyes, hardly flickering at all…a dreaming princess with fantasies of being rescued. She walked passed shops…something for Joe. She was a ghost now, after all, she didn't need to try too hard…no need to win anything.

The Desert-Eyed Young Man who she met a couple of days before stood at the corner. He didn't recognize

Thomas...in his profession he must meet so many people.

Without even being asked, Thomas stepped nearer to Desert-Eyes. "I'm from out of town. I don't have much money, but let me see what's in my pocket."

Desert-Eyes looked startled.

"I didn't mean to scare you." Thomas smiled and stuck her hand in her pocket making a jingling sound. She was now absorbed in her treasure hunt and so was Desert Eyes. Pulling out the contents, she stuffed her keys back in her pocket and held out coins in her hand. The two made eye contact.

His hand like a talon grabbed at the coins, and then with lightning speed he swooped away down the sidewalk where he examined his prize.

Thomas still felt the brush of the man's sharp hand...maybe people get stuck in certain desperate geographies and keep trying to get something that they are afraid they can't live without...like when he was afraid of losing Joe.

She glanced back at Desert Eyes, "Have a nice day honey," and walked on...a present for Joe, that's what she was looking for. Thomas walked further along the side of the street....no more shops...only Tucson, houses with stucco walls gleaming in the sun...barren brown soil, rocks and cacti...something for Joe. She crossed to the other side and walked back towards the shops again...gift shops...the kind of places in which people stop to buy something to prove they've been on vacation…no, better nothing, than just something that doesn't make sense; she kept moving

There, half a block ahead was a shabby sign: *GOODWILL.* She smiled, Goodwill,

what a good idea. The momentum of her steps picked up as if drawn by some

force…how nice the sign was shabby…not part of the world in which things shine

new, slick, seductive, and strangely the same.

The momentum of her steps picked up…she pushed the door open; a bell tinkled, and there she was in Wonderland…the smell of age, a little musty but rich and deep, a smell that no one intended, objects, all different kinds and colors piled on long tables stretching to the back of the store…racks of clothes hanging like memories strung along both walls.

People strolled the aisles casually looking at things, picking them up or trying them on…things they could afford…no frenzy here. This was a graveyard of dreams and a marketplace of possibilities, a reflective place. All these things piled up in rows, things that people once reached for, dear things that people had to strain to buy, the promise of paradise, things to be clasped to the heart. But dreams and things have a way of disappearing, meaning bleeding out and evaporating… maybe this is what time is…the dissolving of desire… not some sort of universal clock, but simply the fading of yearning…very personal. She touched a scratched brass elephant, once desired by someone. Now it sat there, its charisma depleted, waiting patiently for someone to recognize its hidden charms.

Two women no longer young, weight thickening their waists, certainly no longer princesses, picked shirts out of a big pile on a long table. They studied each shirt, examining it carefully, and then either tossed it into a box or gently placed it on a hanger...hardworking women with stories to tell about coming down from towers and facing adversity for which they had not been prepared, exploring mess. Squinting, Thomas tilted his head and could see them shaken and disheveled at the base of their towers, just beginning to get up.

Thomas set off on her casual cruise...something for Joe. Her hand brushed the rainbow rows of cast off clothes...memories like moths flew into the air...no, Joe had his own weird style that Thomas had never quite understood. A whole corner, a barn-like show room was filled with desks and sofas, the sofa's still held the imprints of a of time spent...fossils of long evenings watching television, little stains where someone's delight had spilled over onto the fabric...no, furniture wouldn't do...too hard to carry. She wondered over to a long shelf of lamps...this is more like it...monuments to someone's fancy, strange wonderful ceramic shapes in dreamlike colors...they sat decapitated, only empty sockets where imposing shades had once adorned them...a little too grotesque to give to Joe.

She started sorting through the long tables of smaller miscellaneous objects. Plates, statues, candles, toilet and kitchen accessories, beauty products including combs, pet accessories...a last stop for things that once glittered, having served whatever fanciful purpose for which they were purchased, now buried in this archaeological substrate. Her eyes reflectively coasted over those artifacts...there, right there, an unobtrusive object, almost reluctant to be found...black, like a thousand starless nights, black like that hole she felt when Vance sang...a black, handmade, glazed clay cup, a simple something made at home, a child could have formed it with small unskilled fingers squeezing out a shape of earnest delight. Thomas slowly picked it up...cool... smooth and bumpy all at the same time...black as Silent Night, shiny as all is bright. The cup rested in her hand.

She turned the cup over to check the price...50 cents was roughly scrawled on the unglazed bottom... the bottomless needs of her life, for fifty cents. Why, the creator of this masterpiece had even etched initials, so proud was she of this creation of her hands. The cup sat in Thomas' hand absorbing the heat of her desires and fears...child's play...the small hands forming a thing of beauty out of the stuff of confusion and hurt...this black creation of imagination and beauty holding emptiness... Thomas found herself falling...a hole an absence, a dark battery of life beyond even imagination...letting go of Joe was kind of like that...power...but not a thing or an idea or even a hope. She studied that black cup in her hand, that's what she would give Joe.

A final bus ride to the silent house; her left hand fingered the cool blackness; her right hand pulled the cord. The stores streaming across the windows slowed down...magic. The bus stopped at her corner...the strange chapel across the street...the 60's restaurant glimmered like a shiny beetle in the early afternoon sun. She stood up unnoticed by the other passengers; a green light switched on by the side exit. She gently pushed the doors open and stepped out of that enclosed quiet world and onto the commotion of Broadway. The bus roared away disappearing into that ribbon of commotion stretching out into the Tucson of the future, of which Thomas would not be a part. Her face stopped searching that river of dreams and it looked up to fading mountains quietly watching her.

She turned towards Joe's house; her feet could find their way...her relationship with Joe had always been filled with goodbyes, at least there's not the fear anymore, just a kind of tender sadness echoing somewhere in her stomach, no longer a curse or a punishment...just a reminder of something...what? Her hand snuck into the brown paper bag and caressed Joe's gift...something about blackness and emptiness and haunting beauty and solitude. She nodded slowly; she had tried so hard to win love, a game set to the beat of anticipation and time, and all the while some dark beauty stared out unnoticed, a beauty that was strangely gracious, waiting to embrace her.

She turned the corner and could feel Joe's presence somewhere in the quiet house...Joe sleeping or drinking a beer or painting, his own hand creating something from the confusion of his life...Joe the ghost, fading in and out of geographies of imagination. Thomas put her key in the door, jingling; she turned the key and something silently shifted within the door... it opened.

She stepped in and took the black cup out of the bag and placed it on the coffee table next to *Pride and Prejudice*. Walking into the studio she pulled out her phone, the connection to tomorrow.

"Hello, Danny here."

Thomas began drifting into tomorrow. "Hi darlin'. How ya doin?" Thomas could see Danny on the other end. He was in that dark suit of his, white shirt just beginning to get rumpled, that vigilant sales person's smile on his face...affable and strained, hiding that tenderness and devotion within.

"Busy day here. I met with Marilyn and Gary this morning."

Pause on the other end. "Was it okay?" Thomas' stomach tightened...he stopped the fall into himself and imagined pictures of Danny in trouble, Danny failing, Danny being fired again, fear, fear, fear.

"Sure."

"I'll be back tomorrow evening."

Danny's voice softened. "I miss you."

Thomas stared out the window. "I miss you to." She knew that her voice didn't sound convincing enough. "I do." She ended the call.

Joe walked into the room.

Thomas watched him out of the corner of her eye... this frail aging man who long ago was supposed to save her, the fragile god to whom she made offerings.

Thomas' hand reached over toward the cup. "I looked for something to give you today."

Joe watched Thomas intently.

Thomas spoke slowly as the words materialized in his mind. "I always thought that if somehow I could buy you the right present...the present that would make you see me and fall in love..."

Their eyes flickered between geographies.

Joe was listening.

"Now it all seems kind of strange the way things turned out, but..." She looked down, embarrassed.

"Thomas." Joe whispered.

Thomas looked up. "I could never trust that you cared about me."

Joe looked down speaking softly. "But I did terrible things."

Thomas whispered, "We both did foolish things."

Joe looked up.

"So I looked for a present for you this afternoon... not like old times. When I finally found this weird little cup..." She picked the black cup off the table. "I decided to give it to you, like it had your name on."

Joe looked away, and then anchored his eyes on Thomas and the gift. He took a step closer, his voice soft. "I never needed the gifts. I just wanted to be with you."

Thomas turned back to Joe. "You did?"

"I didn't show it sometimes...I'm glad you could come see me."

Hummingbirds flickered around them.

Joe moved away. "Let me out of here."

Thomas smiled archly; Jane Austen would have been proud of her. "Take your gift, please."

"I don't deserve it."

"It's a gift; not a reward."

No infinities of time, only connection. Two hands exchanged the black cup.

Joe held it for moment, perhaps even feeling the warmth of Thomas' hand.

"You can go now, Joe.

Joe fled to the kitchen.

Chapter 18

S he sat in a narrow seat by the window, the plane sailing east and north, away from the sun, chasing nightfall and cold, as if those wouldn't come soon enough. She glanced at *Pride and Prejudice* sitting listlessly on her lap and then looked out the small rectangle of blue, blue turning to evening and night much faster than she wanted, time condensed by the speed of the plane… funny, she wasn't afraid of being exploded out into the blue, screaming and falling in terror. Joe and the whole crew back in the past of Tucson, fluttering memories… an adventure…stumbling into her kind of adventure… maybe even learning something inside not visible to strangers. She nodded at the window and then looked down at the brown waves of mountains beneath her becoming memories under her very eyes…a little more snow down there.

A blank faced Stewardess pushing a cart stopped by his seat. "What do you want to drink?"

Thomas stared blankly, "Cranberry juice" and looked away...the bitter and the sweet.

The Stewardess mechanically placed a clear plastic cup and a can on Thomas' fragile tray.

Thomas gave her a hummingbird glance.

The Stewardesses hand, without being bidden, deposited a small plastic bag of pretzels next to the can of cranberry juice.

Tender mercies, Thomas' face softened as she turned around and said "Thank you."

She slowly tore the bag open, delicately stuck two fingers into the hole and pulled out one circular pretzel...the round shape was oddly comforting; she hated straight lines. She placed that shape in her mouth; time slowed, then slightly speeded up as her teeth crunched through the pretzel and a sharp taste of salt from condensed oceans and tears began dissolving in her mouth.

She pulled the metallic flap off the can and felt a certain sense of accomplishment. The can felt cold in her hand; ruby colored liquid splashed into the clear plastic cup...how amazing! Pressing the cup to her lips; coldness, sweet and sour coldness flooded her mouth. As the plane rushed towards night she experimented with sequences of drinking and crunching until only empty containers were left on her tray. When The Stewardess walked by holding an empty plastic bag, Thomas picked up the debris of her pleasure and handed it to her with a faint smile.

Thomas pushed the table back up into the seat in front of her and began exploring the worn flight magazine, paging through it. There towards the back was a map showing the paths of all the plane flights. Her finger traced the flight from Tucson to Minneapolis; she looked up startled…the flight lines are curved, they're really curved…slowly her lips curved into a smile…she knew it, just knew it that there was something fishy about that straight line of time and destination.

Now she looked out the window filled with darkness…night…stars above and stars below, no up or down really. Who could be afraid of crashing when there's no direction in which to plummet? Maybe we are like that…no up or down…male or female…stars all around.

That movement into nowhere was disturbed by a subtle shift in speed; the plane ever so slightly pointed downward…yes there was a downward now. The plane sailed on the winds of gravity towards the bright stars below. Those lights increased in size until they illuminated circles of snowy white, and some lights sped along pathways like moving diamond bracelets. Small dark shapes, building and houses stuck up like shadowy mushrooms sprouting from the ground.

The lights inside the plane went off. The plane tilted sideways and dipped downwards spiraling into a black funnel of unknowing. Thomas sat quietly in the darkness in this dizzy initiation to the life she had known. She closed her eyes imagining the arc of the plane flight. The plane engines roared; she felt the plane straighten out. The lights came on. Her eyes opened; she could see the run way now. Half and then another half of the distance from the plane to the ground. Just when she was sure that she was caught in an infinity of half distances, the wheels touching the ground rumbling. The arc of flight made impact, ending on the seemingly flat runway…terrain sped across the small window. Dark figures bundled in coats and breathing out clouds of steam scrambled across the snowy. Huddling protectively against the cold, they tried to complete their tasks as rapidly as possible in the frigid Minnesota night. The plane gradually slowed as it moved along the ground. Thomas could make out the cold face of the person waving signal lights directing the plane toward the gate…the gate…soon Thomas would enter the airport, the gate closing behind her, sealing her off from flight.

All the lights in the plane switched on; a yellow flat brightness solidified objects and people and stories. She and her companions had arrived again at a place of more ordinary compass. An announcement was made telling passengers to remain in their seats until the plane stopped; ordinary desperate people got up from their seats in quiet defiance, eager to join the world of ordinary time. Voices no longer hushed, laughed nervously and talked about plans and weather and jobs. Thomas remained seated, not out of any sense of order; she just needed time…time…was it really time she needed? She retrieved her book that had slipped down between her legs. "As he quitted the room, Elizabeth felt how improbable it was that they should ever see each other again on such terms of cordiality as had marked their several meetings in Derbyshire; and as she threw a retrospective glance over the whole of their acquaintance, so full of contradictions and varieties, sighed at the perverseness of those feelings which now have promoted its continuance, and would formerly have rejoiced in its termination." She whispered, "Perverseness" softly to no one in particular.

The plane came to a complete halt, engines silencing into nothing; overhead bins banged open; each person with ordinary frenzy rushed to get their packs down, rushed to get back to life as they remembered it, a life that looked back and then forward in some imagination of time and hardly noticed the expanse of the moment which opened like a bottomless darkness, terrifying and beautiful.

Thomas sat quietly as the commotion filled the plane...they seemed to be in such a rush, the straight line of time pulling them toward destinations from which soon they would dream of escaping. The refugees were all fleeing now, funneled row after row into the aisle and out of the plane. Thomas just sat there, a look of bewilderment on her face watching ordinary time engulfing the plane...the row in front of her filed into the aisle. Thomas slowly stood up, and softly pulled her knapsack out of the empty bin.

Thomas slung the knapsack over her shoulder, took a deep breath, and began her exit. As she passed The

Stewardess, Thomas nodded. "Thanks for the pretzels; they hit the spot." The Stewardess cocked her head slightly and said in a very smooth professional voice, "I hope you will fly with us again."

Thomas looked at her intensely. "Flying…I hope so."

The Stewardess looked down.

Thomas stepped across the threshold. She could smell the cold as she followed the line of rushing refugees through the enclosed passageway. She stepped out of the passageway through the gate and into a the brilliantly lit airport…people rushing, voices over loud speakers announcing flights and destinations…a flat urgent commotion with so many story lines. Thomas followed the stream of people, familiar strangers down to the baggage terminal and Danny…yes, her life with Danny….her trip slowly being erased from her experience until only the vague track of a dream was left…down the escalator sailing towards the world she left six days ago.

People in ones and twos stepped onto the metal escalator, grooved silver steps carrying a silent line of people downward to be deposited on the ground. Thomas stepped off her metal step onto the floor; she felt the past give her a gentle shove. The people pouring off the escalator dispersed, leaving her standing there with her knapsack on her back. She glanced at her hands, frowned and turned to her right…Danny's silhouette in the distance…Danny's face watching the passengers stream away from the escalator…they saw each other.

Danny winked and flashed his best-devil-may-care smile.

Thomas hesitated slightly trying to hold onto the past.

Danny caught the hesitation.

For a flutter of a second each of them frowned in frustration.

Then hesitation stretched far enough; it snapped back, propelling them into each other's arms. Central Time and Mountain Time merged together as if they had never been apart, two histories began entwining with each other like vines. They hugged.

Danny patted Thomas' back in that nervous way of his. "How was your flight?"

Thomas moved a step back, looking away from Danny's eyes. "I'm not sure where I've been and where I am, but it's good to see you."

Danny glanced away.

Thomas studied his down-turned face, a face on the edge of becoming elderly, a face that could no longer sustain the boy's story of being a hero and the center of excitement.

Now Danny appeared to hesitate. "How about you?"

Thomas gripped the straps of her backpack protectively. "Oh, things were pretty fun." He knew Danny was hungry for a story.

The lines of discontent on Danny's face deepened. "Oh."

"We did a few things." Her backpack gently pulled at her shoulders reminding her of French toasts, Joe's hangdog expression, the faces of all those men, the sad children, the way grapefruits hanging on trees in January and Silent Night...things that don't really fit into Danny or Joe's idea of adventure.

Danny's face brightened; the possibility of a story began. "Was it pretty wild there?"

Thomas raised his eyebrows conspiratorially and smiled mysteriously.

That was enough to prime the pump. "I talked with Bob today. His boyfriend is driving him crazy, and they're going ahead with moving in with each other. I told him it's too soon." He shook his head in knowing silence.

Thomas looked deep in thought...the problem with stories is that they assume there's time and time assumes there's meaning. And everyone from Danny to Jesus, to Buddha, to St. Paul and to Mohamed wants his story to be at the center of the universe...the map that somehow makes the uncertain presence, safe. "You just never know." Thomas nodded noncommittally.

Danny suddenly stopped and became very still. "Genevieve died a couple of days ago.

They both stood there still in the Silent Night moment. Then Danny motioned toward the exit.

Thomas began to follow her partner with appropriate urgency.

Chapter 19

Danny and Thomas started their journey that next Saturday morning, the car winding its way along streets narrowed by tall lumpy piles of snow, piles that grew like living things, each day a little taller. Thomas looked out of the window of the car…Genevieve died at the beginning of the season of winter, the heart of darkness, that hopeless time of year when light and summer and warmth seem outrageous delusions. Thomas frowned at the frigid stasis beyond the glass…a mysterious gap in the seasons during which the angle of the globe hesitates, ambivalent about the sun…time and hope frozen by that indecision. Her reflection in the window held its breath in stillness. Suddenly she took a deep swallow of air and then slowly let it out with relief…yes, she felt it, the ever so slight tilting, the globe beginning to shift its Northern Hemisphere toward the sun. She leaned toward the south to add whatever gravitational influence she possessed.

Danny watched her out of the corner of his eye… what a strange person, his partner, always doing weird little solemn actions, rituals. If Thomas bent forward any farther, her forehead would go through the wind shield…her face seemed frozen in some strange but urgent mystery. "Thomas are you all right?"

Thomas' face grimaced slightly as if she had been interrupted in a very solemn task. She glanced over at Danny and then straightened up…yes, she could still feel that subtle shift to the south. "Sure, do you feel anything different?"

"Different than what?" There was an edge of impatience to Danny's voice.

"The northern hemisphere is just beginning to tilt to the sun."

Danny's eyes remained on the road; his hands tightened on the steering wheel.

Thomas glanced at her partner's face. "Oh I don't know."

Danny continued piloting their course through a gray Minnesota morning.

Thomas' eyes closed…yes, she DID feel it, definitely, that slow tilting toward the sun. She smiled her secret smile.

Danny glanced over at Thomas. He thought that sometimes his partner seemed like one of those deranged Catholic saints that nuns told him about in grade school, Simon something-or-another. He spent the last years of his life seated on top of a column, something to do with a vow to God...such a lonely spectacle. Danny's face flickered from sadness to humor. How in the hell does someone sitting on a pole take a shit? As if in apology he rested his hand gently on Thomas' leg.

Sitting placidly Thomas realized that she had done all she could to bring the sun back...that's when she noticed Danny's hand resting on his leg. The intense solemnity expressed on Thomas' face began to soften. "I wonder what it's like to live without clocks and just have the lengths of days and nights always shifting? I wonder if things would be easier, the changing sky and all?" She turned to Danny expectantly.

Danny nodding with renewed patience, watched the road ahead and the lonely man sitting on the column.

"It would be more democratic."

"Can't trust those Republicans." Danny smiled.

"That's not what I mean." For an instant Thomas frowned forlornly; then she slowly tried again. "It's kind of like the horse-of-a-different-color from the Wizard of Oz. Just having this big mechanical clock measuring everything makes us think that time goes at the same pace for everybody and even worse that everything is measured by that one clock." She struggled with the words. "But you see we're all horses of a different color and every horse is in a world of a different color, and all we have to do is look more closely and the world becomes Technicolor." His voice strained with urgency. "The Clock makes us think that we are all experiencing the same black and white."

His finger resting on Thomas' leg beat out an impatient little rhythm.

Thomas felt the beat and wondered if it was Morse Code. "Does that make sense?"

Danny shrugged his shoulders. "The whole family will be at the funeral."

"Oh."

The two stared out the windshield silently for miles and miles.

Finally the car stopped in front of a barn like building with a skinny wooden cross stuck up like an afterthought on the snow covered, peaked roof. Black suited with a serious look on his face, Danny stepped out of the car. Thomas followed more hesitantly, dressed in the darkest clothes she had.

The two stepped up to the entrance of the church, up a wooden stairway. At the top of which a thin official looking man in a too tight black suite stood sentry. As Danny and Thomas passed him, he dealt them each a funeral program and solemnly motioned them through a double doorway.

Thomas followed Danny into a plain cavernous hall filled with murmuring people. On the far end of the hall an enormous dark, heavy looking metal cross hung, ominously suspended on thin wires; directly beneath it, in harm's way, stood a frail legged white linen covered altar. Thomas paused, wondering how symbols of compassion turn into tools for power.

She took a couple of fast steps to catch up with Danny. Vases of flowers in which white notes were stuck, crowded the altar despite the stark danger from above. On the other end of the hall stood an open coffin in which resided the body of Genevieve. Danny, nodding, shaking hands, merged with that murmuring mass of people; occasionally his profile would stick up out of the crowd, watching out for his partner.

Thomas followed uncertainly in his wake.

Danny would pause in his conversation with someone and look backwards. "Have you met my partner, Thomas?" Thomas would scramble to catch up and stretch out her hand tentatively.

After the third introduction, Thomas drifting irrevocably out of Danny's reach, drew close to the coffin...even with her eyes shut, Genevieve appeared to be listening curiously to the conversations around her, a perfect vantage point; she could be close enough to hear everything but not in the center of the commotion.

In a subtle but sudden shift, people began flowing into pews, the hushed murmurs dissipating.

Danny found Thomas watching Genevieve's body... it was hard to tell which body was more still. Danny stepped next to the two bodies...something in his chest began to stir...funny it seemed to be pushing its way upward. He turned away quickly, "The service is starting."

Thomas, roused from her stillness, turned to her partner and nodded.

Danny led Thomas into the flow; they settled into a wooden pew.

Making herself at home, Thomas took off her coat,

rolling it up like a big sausage, and stuffed it in a corner of the pew. Securely settled next to Danny, Thomas began studying the front of the funeral program. There looking out from its cover sat Genevieve, her face casually resting on her hand as if she were looking out of a window at some interesting scene beyond, eyes open and alert but not penetrating, eyes that wished to create as little disturbance as possible, and yet by their very carefulness suggested peace and strength. Thomas rested her hand comfortingly on Danny's fidgeting hand. Thomas hardly knew Genevieve, she came to their gay wedding; this was before gay weddings were legal. Thomas talked to her for a while a couple of years later when she was beginning to have difficulty swallowing… they talked about the war in Iraq…here she was, her physical abilities diminishing by the minute, facing the moment beyond moments that feels like emptiness. still caring about the events taking place in the broad world around her.

A pink-cheeked minister with thinning blond hair walked up to the pulpit and began speaking smoothly, the words sliding out with solemn sympathy, the way only ministers can. Then hymns and standing and sitting and familiar prayers…finally the family members courageously placed themselves under that huge dark threatening cross hanging from above them to talk about little human episodes in Genevieve's life…a small ordinary life doing the things that ordinary women do in a small ordinary towns. Thomas scratched her head and still…she glanced at Genevieve's picture again…

that curious looking through the window of ordinary time.

A youngish uncertain looking woman with long frizzy haired tied back walked up to the pulpit...Thomas liked her face, a no nonsense face with sharp angles. She stood there for a few moments, head down, feet shuffling a little. When she finally glanced up her eyes looked scared. She took a deep breath and her face firmed up in resolve. As she started speaking her voice became stronger. "This was one of Genevieve's favorite psalms. It's really just a piece of a psalm, a little repeating melody. She liked to sing it, not for anybody...she didn't like audiences; she sang it to herself and to anyone lucky enough to be around, like a lullaby."

The Frizzy Haired Woman froze up for a moment, bewildered by her own audacity. She firmed up again and commenced to speak. "The last time I saw her, she couldn't talk any more. I heard this sound that seemed far away, such a familiar sound, like home beckoning: a song. I stopped and sat there very still to find out where the music was coming from. I even closed my eyes to get a better fix on the sound. When I opened my eyes, I knew it was Genevieve humming. It was that old psalm of hers." The Frizzy Haired Woman took another deep breath and looked out straight and definite at the people in the congregation. "I want to sing it for you, really for Genevieve and her family and myself. It's hard to say goodbye to someone you love. For those of you who heard her sing it, please join in.

The Frizzy Haired Woman cleared her throat.

The mourners fidgeted.

She lifted her head; her eyes looking out into the distance.

Thomas watched her in amazement.

Then miraculously, her deep voice like velvet spread out over the nervous congregation, melody and words together in a lullaby. "Shepard me, O God beyond my wants, beyond my fears, from death to life."

Thomas's lips began silently mouthing the words.

Even though The Frizzy Haired Woman's eyes were red, she seemed happy in some strange end of the world way. She started singing the simple verse again in a kind of intensifying orbit. This time a few scattered voices in the congregation joined her, timidly. "Shepard me, O God, beyond my wants, beyond my fears, from death to life." With each note the simple song drew more voices, snowballing with sadness and something more. Now people sat up straight in their pews, calling out their prayer, calling out to what or whom; it hardly seemed to matter...no destination now but a circle of song, repeating. You couldn't tell who was leading the song...humans calling out with confidence at the brink of something so mysterious and vast, even imagination couldn't echo back, "Shepard me, O God, beyond my wants, beyond my fears, from death to life."

Thomas glanced over at Danny...her partner's chest under that black business man's suite was rising and falling as he called out that plea, tears dripping down from under his glasses down his cheeks.

Chapter 20

After the funeral the car traveled back across the flat snow covered plains; mid-day in a Minnesota winter, a pale lemon sun had just escaped a cloud; in a flicker, the snow glowed, illuminated pearly white from within.

The two sat quietly listening to the hum of the car speeding through the glowing world.

A traffic light set at the intersection of two highways switched to red. Danny's hand quietly slipped into his suite pocket and pulled out a pack of gum. In a feat of incredible dexterity the fingers of one hand delicately pulled a stick of gum from the pack.

He captured Thomas' attention. She stared with the intensity of a bird watcher.

Those magic fingers of Danny's hand peeled the paper off the flat skinny powdery rectangle. The wrapper, released, drifted through time, in slow motion wafting back and forth like a falling leaf before resting on the floor of the car. Sudden as the flicker of humming bird wings, Danny slipped the gum into his mouth. Even he seemed surprised at the magic of it all and began chewing with relish. He looked over at Thomas. "I bet you never saw anyone do that before."

Thomas entranced by the feat, nodded, lost in the wonder of it all.

Danny's hand gracefully tilted the pack of gum toward Thomas. "Do you want a piece?"

The traffic light switched from red to green as fast as a flickering wing. She turned to Danny, "Yes." She delicately picked out a stick of gum.

Still pleased with himself, Danny said, "That Genevieve was a real lady."

Thomas chewed his gum and nodded with satisfaction.

The End